Breaking Open the Box

Breaking Open the Box

A Guide for Creative Techniques to Improve Academic Writing and Generate Critical Thinking

Nancy Dafoe

ROWMAN & LITTLEFIELD EDUCATION

A division of
ROWMAN & LITTLEFIELD PUBLISHERS, INC.
Lanham • New York • Toronto • Plymouth, UK

Published by Rowman & Littlefield Education
A division of Rowman & Littlefield Publishers, Inc.
A wholly owned subsidiary of The Rowman & Littlefield Publishing Group, Inc.
4501 Forbes Boulevard, Suite 200, Lanham, Maryland 20706
www.rowman.com

10 Thornbury Road, Plymouth PL6 7PP, United Kingdom

British Library Cataloguing in Publication Information Available

Library of Congress Cataloging-in-Publication Data

Dafoe, Nancy, 1952–
Breaking open the box : a guide for creative techniques to improve academic writing and generate critical thinking / Nancy Dafoe.
pages cm
Includes bibliographical references.
ISBN 978-1-4758-0273-3 (cloth : alk. paper)—ISBN 978-1-4758-0274-0 (pbk. : alk. paper)— ISBN 978-1-4758-0275-7 (electronic) 1. English language—Rhetoric—Study and teaching. 2. Academic writing—Study and teaching. 3. Critical thinking—Study and teaching. I. Title.
PE1404.D34 2013
808'.0420711—dc23

2012044863

∞™ The paper used in this publication meets the minimum requirements of American National Standard for Information Sciences—Permanence of Paper for Printed Library Materials, ANSI/NISO Z39.48-1992.

Printed in the United States of America

Contents

Foreword

I had the good fortune of meeting Nancy Dafoe fifteen years ago when she enrolled in my graduate seminar on the teaching of writing. I still remember the poignant memoir she wrote for the first assignment. It described the afternoon she rummaged through her grandmother's second-floor bedroom and was stunned to discover the memorabilia of an uncle she knew nothing about. Her uncle Bob had died in World War II at the age of twenty-two, and over the years, her family suppressed the painful memory.

I find it fitting that Nancy has written *Breaking Open the Box* because she has an invaluable insider's point of view. She is an award-winning poet and fiction writer, a talented academic writer, and a highly acclaimed teacher of writing at both the high school and college levels. Nancy will be the first to tell you that her writing informs her teaching. "Being a writer helps me to understand students' struggles with writing," she says, "and I think I am a more patient teacher as a result of my own experiences. I also think being a writer helps me to break down assignments for students in a meaningful way to help them master and apply writing techniques." In this book, we learn much from Nancy's knowledge of teaching combined with her insights about writing.

As the director of a large writing program at the State University of New York at Cortland, an author of four textbooks on academic writing, and a professor of English education, I am particularly pleased that Nancy has written this book. Over the past thirty years, I've observed many uninspiring classroom lessons on writing, and I've read countless mind-numbing student essays. I have rarely encountered teachers who create classrooms in which students flourish as writers, and I have seldom read original student essays that move creatively from introduction to conclusion. *Breaking Open the Box* offers an instructional approach that has the potential to change this picture. By incorporating creative writing pedagogy into the academic writing classroom, we will be able to offer effective, stimulating lessons that give our students the strategies they need to write with verve and voice.

In *Breaking Open the Box,* Nancy offers guidance on how to transform our classrooms into writing communities by allotting more time to sustained writing practice, offering scaffolded instruction in creative techniques, teaching writing in tandem with reading, using professional and student models as touchstone texts, and inspiring students with supportive flexibility and positive choice. Nancy's action research and the student work she includes in this book suggest that these changes will empower students, engage them in the writing process, make them more alert critical thinkers, and give them an increased understanding of reading assignments.

The time is ripe for the fresh approach in *Breaking Open the Box* because we face formidable challenges on two fronts. We are struggling to prevent standardized testing from draining creativity out of our classrooms. At the same time, we are grappling with Common Core State Standards (CCSS) that require us to assign more nonfiction "informational" texts and text-based academic writing. As we contend with these forces, we have to choose our tactics carefully.

If we focus on academic writing (chiefly exposition and argument) at the expense of expressive writing (narration and description), we run the risk of producing reluctant, apathetic readers and bored, disengaged writers. I see these students every day in college composition classes. They read perfunctorily and write mechanically. They simply regurgitate the information they find in their reading sources, and they attempt to mimic stodgy prose that is devoid of style and voice. Nancy shows us how to avoid this potential risk by assigning powerful, well-written texts and teaching students to read as writers. The objective is to identify an author's rhetorical devices and analyze the effects they have on the reader. This is different from the reading done in a traditional English class. And the student writing is different still. Students experiment with select creative techniques in their own essays after examining the effect a particular device can have on their readers, asking, for example, What if I added narration in the form of an anecdote? What if I included a descriptive scene? What if I inserted a metaphor? By teaching critical reading and academic writing in tandem, *Breaking Open the Box* demonstrates that academic writing and creative writing don't have to be in opposition to each other. Academic writing leaves room for creativity.

At a time when we are preoccupied with assessment and state standards, some of us may be jittery about devoting class time to creativity.

Nancy assuages our fears. She offers a number of rubrics that show that creative efforts can easily and effectively be evaluated, and in chapter 14 she shares her thoughts on how instruction in creative choice and creative techniques meets the Common Core State Standards.

The Common Core State Standards represent writing as "informational," "argumentative," and "text-based." But the CCSS do not prevent us from teaching students to make academic writing vigorous and energetic by adding creative techniques. In fact, the CCSS recommend "text exemplars" that include the same creative devices that Nancy promotes in this book. Consider Amy Tan's "Mother Tongue" with its dialect and amusing linguistic vignettes; Anna Quindlen's "A Quilt of a Country" with its extended metaphor and personal examples; and Robert Preston's *The Hot Zone*, a nonfiction account of an Ebola virus outbreak that contains narrative devices that make it as terrifying and suspenseful as a Stephen King novel. Tan, Quindlen, and Preston back up their arguments with facts, research, and reason, but they also employ creative writing devices that favor first-person pronouns, descriptive details, dialogue, stories, examples, asides, similes, metaphors, and personification. This is the type of writing we want our students to emulate.

With energy and flair, Nancy Dafoe argues that *creative academic writing* can be taught, and she offers many helpful suggestions, tools, strategies, and model student texts that will enable us to do so. She describes how to set the stage for good writing by establishing a respectful environment in which students are willing to take risks, share experiments with risk taking with their peers, and provide constructive feedback. She guides us through the process of workshopping, having students read, share, and give feedback to their peers' works-in-progress and having teachers conduct student conferences.

If we teach our students the nuts and bolts of academic writing but tell them nothing about the actual craft of writing, we will continue to collect boring, predictable essays that put all of us to sleep. We need to break open the box and give our students the tools they need to invigorate their writing with catchy leads, dramatic sentences, narrative stance, and well-placed metaphors and similes. We need to teach *creative academic writing*.

Breaking Open the Box belongs on the shelf of every secondary school and college teacher of writing. Crack it open and begin giving your students the writing instruction they deserve.

Dr. Mary Lynch Kennedy
Distinguished Teaching Professor of English
Director of Composition and Campus Writing
State University of New York at Cortland

Preface: Writing Well Matters

> Teaching our students to write expressively and well may be the most valuable lesson we can offer.

Pick up any newspaper, read a blog on contemporary mores and culture, skim a job applicant's letter of introduction, listen to a political speech or even a written declaration of love at a wedding, and you might find yourself cringing at our collective inarticulateness.

Writing is integral to every aspect of our lives, yet we are surrounded by examples of bad writing that do not convey the intended messages. While reading or listening to these poor examples of writing, we may wince at the writers' linguistic attempts at gymnastics that cost job opportunities, alienate part of the audience, or produce unnecessary tensions, and we consider the myriad costs of living in a society of individuals who struggle to write well.

Educator and leader in composition studies David Bartholomae noted, "Writing problems are also social and political problems."[1] We are not helpless, however; educators can work together to help our students produce better writing, writing that better expresses the growing sophistication of their ideas.

Breaking Open the Box is designed to help teachers and college professors/writing instructors teach students to improve their academic writing by giving them more direct responsibility in the decision-making processes, by providing opportunities for them to explore creative techniques in their writing, and by encouraging creative frameworks for their rhetoric.

It is not simply about incorporating creative techniques in writing instruction, however. This strategic writing instruction is aimed at helping students build the skills necessary to make creative choices in every stage of the writing process.

This text is the result of fourteen years of teaching practice in the area of English language arts (ELA) at the secondary level, teaching English composition at a community college, action research, a number of years of a career in journalism and public relations, and creative writing in poetry, fiction, and essay.

The union of high school and college course teaching assignments initially led to an examination of the most effective strategies and teaching practices that resulted in the greatest improvements in students' academic writing.

The techniques suggested in this text work at all levels of secondary education and college instruction. Students have repeatedly attested to the fact that the reading and writing experiences outlined in this text have helped to make them more skilled and confident writers.

Experience in both the high school and college environments helped to identify and codify the problems students face, those problems being not part of one system or another but related to widespread instructional approaches and unease with or unawareness of how creativity enhances the writing process, not just the product.

The division—between the writing applications in what some students have called the "fun" English classes and the rigors of academic writing demanded in the college preparatory or college writing courses—is an artificial one and does not benefit students. The shape of the writing assignments often speaks more to instruction practices than to student learning.

Alluding to Hamlet's soliloquy, "the play's the thing," in this context, the shape is too often the thing in writing instruction, perhaps because it is the easiest to define and imitate. The content should, however, be our aim as writers and as writing instructors.

When our students tell us that, for the first time, they feel like writers, we know we are doing something right. But we need to examine those practices and make sure that we can duplicate the experiences in order to allow every student to come to that "aha!" moment when he or she discovers the power of a conceit or the multiple levels of meaning found in carefully crafted diction.

Along similar lines, creative writing students have frequently stated in their end-of-semester evaluations that they were proud of their writing as a revelatory experience. When asked why in the surveys, they wrote that they felt personally invested in their poems, stories, and other expressions of their ideas, repeatedly offering some form of the statement, "It doesn't feel like something I just wrote for a teacher."

Why don't all students feel this way about their writing? Educators know how much time high school teachers and college professors invest in preparation, lesson planning, and teaching only to have students hate their academic written products. When students despise their work, they typically spend very little time on that material.

Not surprisingly, we work at what we value. One significant problem is that our students too seldom take ownership of their written products, let alone see their writing as defining in any way.

We need to teach not only the skills, charged Mina Shaughnessy, according to educator David Bartholomae, but "also an understanding of text and purpose, so that the act of writing could enable students . . . to begin their lives anew."[2] Writing is about discovery, learning, and, yes, identity. Yet it is readily apparent to most educators that the majority of students do not identify themselves as writers.

This concept is more basic and more urgent than the statements arising out of discussions about the Common Core Standards of Readiness. While Common Core should, ultimately, improve education, we know that teaching creative techniques and encouraging creative choice have improved student writing and fostered higher levels of critical thinking as well as closer attention to texts.

If you are not sure if your students see themselves as writers, try this in-class activity that has been widely shared with teachers in workshops: Give your students index cards and ask them to write down ten nouns or adjectives that describe who they are. Tell them that they have only thirty seconds to record their identifiers. Then discuss with them what they wrote. How many of your students wrote the word "writer" as a descriptor? How many wrote the word "reader"?

If our students don't see themselves as readers and writers, it is unlikely that they will value the critical skills needed to write well and read analytically. The few students who define themselves as readers and/or writers are likely to be good students. It is not coincidental.

The students who are most willing to take creative risks with writing begin to identify themselves as writers more readily than those students who seldom, if ever, take creative risks. Students who do not see themselves as writers but follow the rules in order to obtain a higher grade are often disengaged with the content of their academic work even if they are concerned about the grade. They will very honestly state, "I'm just doing this to graduate."

Although we could speculate on the relationship between creative freedom and improvements in writing based upon observations, more immediate and objective data is available in the form of surveys that the students fill out before and after their writing assignments, as well as the formal assessments in writing.

Developed as part of action research, the survey analysis helps us move from anecdotal ascertainment to data-specific conclusions that can be objectively verified. From earlier informal observations, I noticed specific patterns, but I knew that I needed to quantify those perceptions with a more formal and systematic approach if I was to duplicate the students' successes with writing applications.

Initially, the action research began in one classroom, and then I widened the testing pool. The results of the two-year action research project consistently demonstrated what logic would tell us: students who have more say in what and how they write are more invested in their products, and students who feel engaged with their writing are more likely to take the time necessary to edit and revise their work.

In addition, students who practice creative techniques enter texts with greater curiosity, and their writing reflects a deeper level of thinking about the essential questions of the topics.

Because this approach encourages student choice and student-initiated creative design to writing and reading, the point of the instruction is not the technique but the practice of process writing. Initially discomforting to some students, creative approaches work because the student must examine texts more carefully and consider the frame for the written analysis from multiple angles.

There are no simple questions, short responses, or pat answers to open-ended writing tasks in this methodology. By the nature of creative approaches to writing tasks, the element of "rigor" is inherent in the process rather than supplemental, but the approach also requires more flexibility from teachers.

Educators know that writing and identity are inextricably linked. If we struggle to communicate, to articulate our ideas and feelings, our sense of self is, in some measure, diminished. In examining how our own writing skills began to advance, we can look back at early examples of compositions and see points of divergence.

Writing improves dramatically after we become aware of the rules, cognizant of how various techniques may be best used, and then we begin to deliberately break some of the rules with a clear understanding of what effect those choices have on our readers. At some point, good writers realize that they have to learn not to be cautious—and compliant—if their writing is to become more successful, address an imperative, make a persuasive argument, and better engage the audience.

This is the self-realization through which we want to guide our students.

A wonderful quotation that complements this imperative may be found in Annie Dillard's *The Writing Life*:

> One of the things I know about writing is this: spend it all, shoot it, play it, lose it, all, right away, every time. Do not hoard what seems good for a later place in the book or for another book; give it, give it all, give it now. The impulse to save something good for a better place later is the signal to spend it now. Something more will arise for later, something better.[3]

Dillard's statements suggest the urgency behind writing, as well as the dynamics of the written words. The musing on a quotation model works just as well in an English composition class in which college freshmen initially appear at a loss over what to write as it does in a high school classroom.

When a student identifies himself or herself as a writer, everything changes for that developing scholar. Writing becomes not a chore but self-expression. Almost every professional writer recalls the moment when the concept of self became conflated with that of a writer.

Roger Rosenblatt wrote about this moment in an essay published in the *New York Times Sunday Book Section*: "I loved living in a mystery. Thus, though I hardly knew it at the time, I was becoming a writer."[4] Recognizing the self as writer is tremendously affirming.

Writing should not feel like a foreign language or a subject for which most students have no entry, and yet, sadly, that is exactly how many students feel by the time they leave high school.

Virginia Woolf speaks to this concept of including or alienating readers in her concluding line in "The Modern Essay" from *The Common Reader*: "A good essay must have this permanent quality about it; it must draw its curtain round us, but it must be a curtain that shuts us in not out."[5] We should reflect on this quotation when we talk with students who appear to feel shut out of the dialogic, the exchange of ideas expressed in writing.

Recently, college students in an English 099 course confessed to a kind of writing paralysis that froze them, the result of years of a feeling of failure to articulate their ideas. Teachers and students alike need to change what we do to alleviate that frustration and the perception that writing is some exercise for the elite.

We want all students to see themselves as writers and readers. When that transformation happens, the actualization of scholarship in writing as well as in other disciplines follows naturally.

This book was not written to fill the requirements of a master's or PhD program; rather, it is the culmination of years of frustration with student products and scoring in that old equation of student-writer equals teacher-grader. It is also the result of listening to students discuss what will help as well as what must be overcome in order to find the path to better writing.

Students will admit to the fact that many of them spend very little time reflecting on or composing their written products for school. This observation is as true in a tenth-grade ELA class as it is in a college comp classroom.

A number of young MFA (master's of fine arts) graduate students at the Association of Writers and Writing Programs (AWP) annual conference noted that their experiences with their students in freshman comp classes and seminars indicated exactly the same type of behaviors and poor products that high school teachers are seeing.

The idea of blaming one group or another seemed tremendously counterproductive. The solution will not be found through college teachers blaming high school teachers or high school teachers blaming middle school teachers and so on. We all need to own the problem and then work toward solutions that include students' voices in the conversation. Students are more than willing and ready to tell us that many of them feel they have no control, no interest, and no stake in their own education.

With few exceptions, educators become teachers and professors for noble reasons, but the outmoded, industrial model of secondary school public education in the United States makes it difficult for innovators to offer creative approaches to writing instruction and learning.

Likewise, students are unable to continue at a university or college until they have passed the English comp course, and the strain on both the student and the instructor is often severe.

It is our students, however, who pay the highest price for the politics and lack of creativity in many of our classrooms. The politicization of educational reform has nearly everyone focused on testing and data collection—not the best environment for experiments in writing in which "failure" is an important part of the process and necessary for real improvements.

Other types of pressures restrict creative freedoms for the college comp professors or adjunct instructors of freshmen writing seminars. In their text "What Can Academic Writers Learn from Creative Writers?" Maria Antoniou and Jessica Moriarty argue in their abstract, "Creative Writing lecturers hold valuable knowledge on the writing process, which is currently underutilized in Higher Education."[6]

While we may wholeheartedly agree with Antoniou and Moriarty, I suspect that the creative writing instructors' knowledge about process is underutilized partially because that knowledge is frequently undervalued in higher education. It is also very likely undervalued in the secondary education classroom.

Yet the direct link between creativity and critical thinking that even the new College and Career Readiness Anchor Standards have recognized is demonstrated in creatively written products.

Writing is more than a tool for expression; it is either the entrance or exit door. Excellent, skillful, grammatically correct writing offers an entrance. We will return to this metaphor because academically weaker students have often stated that they feel like they are outsiders in this system. Too many feel that they will never be able to be part of this conversation of scholarly writers and readers.

Crediting Mina Shaughnessey with the concept, Bartholomae stated in *Writing on the Margins*, "Teach not only skills but also an understanding of context and purpose, so that the act of writing could enable students . . . to begin their lives anew."[7] We want our students to begin their "lives anew" as they are elevated by the act of writing well.

This text offers teachers and college writing instructors a different way of looking at instruction, not simply a series of lesson plans or workshop strategies. Because the approach may be taken in any classroom and incorporated in any writing lesson, it is widely applicable and, with tailoring, will fit every educator who has an interest in improving student writing.

Borrowing from author Malcolm Gladwell in his book *Blink*, "Once we know about how the mind works—and about the strengths and weaknesses of human judgment—it is our responsibility to act."[8] And we have discovered that offering more creative choice in writing instruction, providing many and varied opportunities for students to explore language play in writing, as well as direct instruction in writing techniques, changes how our students think about the world, about themselves, about text complexity, and about expressing their ideas.

It is our responsibility to act.

Acknowledgments

My sincerest gratitude is extended to State University of New York (SUNY) Cortland College Distinguished Teaching Professor Dr. Mary Lynch Kennedy for her interest in and advice on writing this book; my friend, poet, and fellow educator Gwynn O'Gara; SUNY Cortland Distinguished Teaching Professor Karla Alwes; and East Syracuse Minoa (ESM) Central School District Superintendent Dr. Donna Desiato.

I would like to thank my ESM High School English Department friend and colleague Maureen Watkins, who conducted teacher action research with me; my friends and English teacher colleagues Cindy Hlywa, Amanda Smith, Jennifer Kirchoff, Jeffrey Scheiwiller, and Margaret Newell, who read early drafts of my book and offered suggestions and comments; my college creative writing professor, early mentor, and friend Professor William Rosenfeld; my first readers/editors and daughters, Colette Dafoe and Nicole Dafoe; and my husband, Daniel Dafoe, for his patience and endless encouragement. I'd also like to thank Dr. Thomas F. Koerner and Carlie Wall at Rowman & Littlefield Education.

I must also thank all of my wonderful high school and college students, who have continued to inspire me, particularly those noted here, who offered to contribute to this text with their writing or helped me generate creative ideas for teaching writing, in alphabetical order: Brett Adams, Laura Adams, Mark Adams, Jenna Ballard, Katrina Ballard, Derek Bowers, David Bray, Kara Button, Carolyn Byrd, Kazimieras Celiesius, Alex Cole, Asa Cole, Charles Davidson, Kourtney Day, Brett Dearstine, Alexander J. DePietro, John Winters DiMarco, Christie Donato, Alexandra Durantini, Jake Ezzo, Olivia Fecteau, Claire Ferris, Nicholas Finch,

Mason Fiore, Selena Fiore, Madeline Fowler, Cassie Gorman, Sarah Goyer, Kimberly Halligan, Samantha Harmon, Tricia Honors, William Imperiale, Amanda Jaquin, Riley Johnson, Hilary Kates, Maggie Kates, Allison Kuklinski, Kara LaBarge, Christian Larrabee, Thomas Marini, Ian Marsh, Sarah Marsh, Olivia Martin, Michael McKean, Jillian Mitchell, Jhad Mozeb, Mushtak Mozeb, Michael Mullane, Steven Mullane, Ryan Murphy, Minh Nguyen, Adam Ott, Trevor Pokrentowski, Angelica Popp, Alec Raphael, Andrea Riedman, Michelle Riedman, Andres Rodriguez, Kevin Rogers, Julia Shipley, Emer Stack, Parker Stone, Brian Sweeney, Devin Sweeney, Sean Sweeney, Shannon Sweeney, Megan Terry, Emily Thompson, Andrew Troast, Molly Voss, Erik Waltz, Kylie Waltz, Jackie Waltz, Charlotte Visser, and Haley Wodarczyk. There is no book without all of you.

Introduction: The Approach, the Heart of the Matter, the Structure

We're ready to break open the restrictive boxes to help our students become better writers. Where to begin? The relationship between writing creatively and critical thinking is explored in chapter 1 and expanded upon in chapter 2, as the creative writer begins playing with language, taking calculated risks in order to improve his or her rhetoric.

Chapter 3 acknowledges the problems inherent in a fluid form such as the essay genre and why its various and glorious permutations cause such difficulty for young writers. This chapter also addresses what goes wrong when a typically good student writes a vacuous essay, as well as what goes amazingly right when a weaker academic student produces a surprisingly good piece of writing. Creativity is always at the center of this positive experience for the student and teacher.

Although this is a text designed for educators, it is student-centered with student products at its heart. As educators examine the students' language play, metaphoric riffs, and narrative frameworks for their rhetoric in chapters 4 through 11, we can begin to envision how this methodology demands far more from students at the same time that it rewards them with greater engagement in their writing.

Educators have an opportunity in chapters 4 through 11 to see how students work through analytical problems—presented by difficult texts—by using creative designs and creative language. By design, chapters 4 through 11 contain the centerpiece of *Breaking Open the Box* because educators need to see how a particular creative framework or creative technique leads the student to divergent thinking, to analysis in ways that might not have been considered prior to the writing process.

The expansive section on teaching metaphors and encouraging students to try to use metaphoric language in their essays takes up the lion's share of chapter 4 because writing with metaphors seems to have the greatest impact on improving not only student writing but critical thinking. It is also a technique that may be used by students experimenting with creative frameworks.

In many respects, the emphasis on teaching the metaphor to improve both writing and reading of dense texts was student-initiated. Students' ability to see how working with metaphoric language changed not only their writing but their thinking came as a surprise to them, and they expressed that honestly and lyrically.

The students here make the choices for their arguments, and educators may determine which ones are the most intriguing to them and their classroom practices. Student applications with narrative, parody, musings, and journaling may be used by teachers to model technique or the design of a written argument.

Each assignment offered in this text, by way of example, focuses on a specific goal; for example, incorporating metaphors in writing in order to better understand characterization in a work of literature. How the student meets those goals is up to him or her, fostering scholarly independence, a skill that remains with the students who seek it out long after they have left formal schooling.

The greatest difficulty in compiling the material for chapters 4 through 11 was deciding which student-submitted writing products to leave out of the text. There were so many students who wanted to share what they had learned about academic writing, using creative techniques and creative approaches, that the book would have literally burst open if all of them were included.

Chapters 4 through 11 focus on different creative frameworks or creative techniques used by the students in analyzing the literature. The rationale for exploration of various vehicles for argument is discussed in the preface, but it is worth reiterating here: when students have the option of choosing the structures for their rhetoric, they take greater ownership of the products.

After seeing the results of the student products in chapters 4 through 11, educators wanting to design assignments and/or assessments that encourage creativity will find support for that process in chapters 12 through 16.

While every teacher knows that editing and revision are tremendously important stages of the writing process, we also know how reluctantly students take up these tasks, as discussed in chapter 13. When our students are actively engaged in their written products, they make the time necessary to revise and edit. Chapter 13 addresses this correlation and the conclusions reached as a result of action research projects.

Chapter 14 addresses the new Common Core Standards for College and Career Readiness, specifically examining the language of these standards that advocates for student-initiated creative choices in academics. This chapter helps to alleviate some of our fears that trying a new and creative approach to teaching writing will be in some way at odds with the learning standards. In fact, chapter 14 demonstrates the opposite.

Advocating creative choice for educators, as well as for students, we have a very short chapter on setting up lesson plans that incorporate creative choice. A few sample rubrics are also included in chapter 15 in order for teachers to see how a specific writing task might address the evaluation of students' creative choice or application of creative techniques.

The action research conducted for this book indicates a strong correlation between time spent revising and student investment in the work. Chapter 16 outlines an approach to setting up an action research design for your own classroom. It is not an intimidating process, but rather one in which you can see the direct results of your teaching practices verified by the data. While there are many ways in which our research can be organized, the steps listed in this chapter are very easy to follow and allow anyone to duplicate the positive results.

After all of the wonderful student products your students will write—as a result of these strategies—it only makes sense to include a short chapter on providing students with opportunities for reaching an authentic audience. Chapter 17 suggests ways in which we can give our students a voice beyond the classroom.

Mirroring the creative approaches found in the student-writing sections of *Breaking Open the Box,* the dedication at the end of this book offers an unusual and creative approach to instruction, with each poem representing both an individual student and a term integral to literary analysis. Taken together, the poems make up a classroom of students and approaches to the study of literature. We begin to recognize that creativity is not only beneficial to our students but to our teaching practices as well.

All of the exercises in writing outlined in this text build skills, so students will be able to bring their new skill set and greater command of language to formal assessments (i.e., essays) and, ultimately, to oral and written communications in their careers and lives.

1

Encouraging Creative Frameworks for Critical Thinking and Writing

> The vehicle for the message is less important than the concepts contained in that agent.

Dan Beachy-Quick writes musings on the line, the language of classification, the ocean, as well as poems on Ahab and the mouth of the whale in *A Whaler's Dictionary*, a text uneasily cast as journal, prose poem, musing, and essay delving into the waters of Herman Melville's *Moby Dick*.[1]

David Foster Wallace began his essay "Tense Present: Democracy, English, and the Wars over Usage" with a litany—as in tedious account—of phrases made up of poor usage, the grammatically incorrect, and unintentional, awkward puns.[2] Pico Iyer writes in "In Praise of the Humble Comma" that punctuation is like "the gods, they say, give breath, and they take it away."[3]

While lyrical and immensely creative, Beachy-Quick's text is also a fine analytical work on the literature of Melville. When we finish reading his book, we are tempted to run to get a copy of *Moby Dick*, a work many of us have not read since high school. The fact that Beachy-Quick's language is gorgeous adds to rather than detracts from the heuristic nature of the work that causes the reader to search more deeply in Melville's literature. Although *A Whaler's Dictionary* does not *look* like analysis, it is acutely keen analysis.

Nor does Wallace's essay resemble anything approaching an essay form until about four pages into the text, and even then, the reader is uncertain until the seventh page, at which point Wallace uses the heading

"Thesis Statement for Whole Article," following a half-page footnote with an editor's note, sardonically suggesting a verbal battle with the editor.[4]

Iyer personifies punctuation in a playful manner with a serious undertone that speaks to the importance of mechanics to our very cultural identity. As Iyer states, "A world that has only periods is a world without inflections. It is a world without shade. It has a music without sharps or flats. It is a martial music."[5]

What does the creative interiority of Beachy-Quick's "dictionary" or Wallace's idiosyncratic "article," or even Iyer's personification of the comma have to do with teaching students academic writing? The answer is "Everything."

For all of the attention supposedly paid to Bloom's "new" taxonomy—with creativity ranked at the very top—educators tend to be shy about introducing creative writing techniques in the college English composition and secondary school classrooms where traditional analysis and the objective style and tone of the literary critic reign supreme. It is as if we all secretly and fearfully agreed with Conrad Aiken's ironic line 23 in his poem "The Room" that creativity brings "back chaos out of shape."[6]

Whether it is because of the pressure arising out of high-stakes testing in the high school classroom, the politicization of education, or the nature of the difficulty of change, both college composition and secondary school teachers seem to have adopted the critic's framework, that formal tone and structure so despised by Samuel Johnson in his essay "The Critic," in which he refers to literary criticism as "a study by which men grow important and formidable at a very small expense."[7]

We do not really want our students to write like the inane critics referred to in Johnson's work, but we unintentionally set our students up for this inevitability with the formats we teach and the drills we have them repeatedly practice. Even more troubling, however, is that we set them up to detest their written work, resulting in a spiraling decrease in interest in writing.

Our students know structures, however. When asked, nearly every secondary school student and college freshman—even the academically weakest ones—will tell you that an essay is made up of five paragraphs (until they learn otherwise), including an introduction and conclusion. They will very likely repeat a mantra about topic and supporting sentences.

Beyond this rudimentary framework, however, they seem to struggle with the permutations of the form, clarity of meaning, and relevance of texts, whether that text is fiction or nonfiction. In other words, they understand format but not content. They think they know what an essay should look like without having any clear idea of what an essay is.

Generally, students have received excellent instruction in composition and essay structures through multiple years of practice and direct instruction in school, but these same students are lost when it comes to filling those vessels with something meaningful or worth reading. Students and teachers alike will attest to the generally sad state of the student essay.

Still, there is not enough documentation and articulation of these connections to make everyone comfortable with the idea that instruction in creative techniques will enhance not only writing and writing processes but also critical thinking.

For an organizational guide to teaching composition, Thomas Newkirk's *Nuts and Bolts: A Practical Guide to Teaching College Composition* is a great text for instructors of both college comp courses and high school English classes, but for exploration into how to move struggling students beyond the formulas to more meaningful and better content, other approaches and texts are sorely needed.

This is where *Breaking Open the Box* comes into the discussion. The incorporation of creative techniques and creative choice within the English and college composition curricula may make some instructors uneasy at first because the approach outlined here asks instructors to give up some of the decisions we make and turn them over to our students. The results, however, are well worth the risks associated with these nontraditional methodologies.

Elementary educators have long favored creativity in the classroom, encouraging students to practice creative writing without teaching techniques, but somewhere in the journey through twelve to thirteen years of schooling, students have come to bury their creativity either by accident or design.

The movement away from children's natural creative impulses to a direction in which they fit their writing into the frameworks of shapes and boxes, quite literally, is a gradual one, purportedly taught to instill academic discipline and the look of academic writing, but it is also designed to facilitate the ease and speed with which student product can be assessed and scored.

We all know high school teachers and college professors who have experimented with creative writing projects in which students' writing takes various shapes, and we have repeatedly heard the comment, "Why do I do this to myself?" The answer, of course, is because it is worth it. What advantage does instruction in creative techniques bring to students struggling with academic writing? One answer is entrance.

The process of finding creative vehicles for arguments, the tasks of searching for metaphoric language that best expresses an idea allow reader and writer to explore texts more deeply and in myriad ways. Creative approaches and unusual frameworks for written arguments necessitate spending more time with both reading and writing, resulting in a higher level of scholarship.

One student recently related that he had to go back to the novel and read and reread passages many times before he could figure out how he wanted to creatively approach the task. Allowing choice and encouraging creativity actually causes students to take greater ownership and discourages pat or superficial responses.

In addition, creative technique applications often launch divergent thinking, leading to innovations in areas beyond writing. Creative writers become creative thinkers and better readers. This creative approach toward learning works if we allow that student "products" are still in the development stage and that writing is a process. Imagine if every word professional educators wrote was held up as a final "product."

There seems to be general apprehension about challenging students to do more when too often they choose to do less than the required reading and writing. The shifts in our culture are apparent. Young people feel so many pulls away from reading texts and writing. Recognizing those pulls and figuring out how to bring students back into the conversation is the beginning.

What we will discover by following the methodology outlined in this text is that in asking students to do more, allowing them to make the kind of choices that are often annexed by instructors, our students will surprise us by beginning to seek out opportunities even without the prompting of educators.

Giving students these creative challenges empowers them, as student John Stone* wrote so concisely: "Before being in your class, I enjoyed English, but I never considered myself to be a good writer. Encouraging me to write creatively gave me confidence in experimenting with my essays and decreased the fear of failure."[9]

Paradoxically, John noted that experimenting with writing decreases rather than increases a fear of failure in writing, and the improvement in his writing over the course of the year demonstrated that his willingness to experiment with his writing also extended its power.

Another high school student, a senior, wrote a particularly revealing and pertinent note in her free-writing journal in a creative writing class:

> Creative writing is such a breath of fresh air for an English class. Instead of reading a multitude of pages at 11 p.m. and still missing the point of the assignment, we research what is relevant to the topic in this class. In addition, creative writing is so pleasantly out-of-the-box. There are no structure restrictions to hold my ideas back. While I often feel caged and blind in other classes, I am flowering with life in this class. There are no mind games (trying to understand the directions while fitting into a piece of a puzzle the teacher will mold). The well-needed release that comes from this class gives me hope that when I enter the real world, I will still have creativity left to share.

If we give our students the opportunities, they will help to write the plan for improving their writing. In other words, if we encourage them, they will tell us what is holding them back. They will offer responses as to what will allow them to make the exciting kind of progress we all want for them. They are asking their teachers how the processes we teach are as critical as the information we provide.

We want our students to walk out into the world with their creativity flourishing, their decision making and critical thinking developing, and their writing precisely and distinctly expressing their ideas. Allowing them more creative freedom to design writing assignments and to construct the frameworks for their arguments and more choices in the exposition will lead to improved results. It is time to give our students back their creative voices and open doors for their creative choices, as well as expect so much more from them.

SUMMARY NOTES

Allowing students choice in creating a framework for their academic arguments will lead to both higher levels of performance and more time spent on writing tasks, resulting in better editing, fewer errors, and improved products.

2

The Writer as Creative Thinker

SECTION 1: PLAYING WITH LANGUAGE

One of the skills that provide teachers insight into students' frustration with their rhetoric is essay writing. Unfortunately, few students see the essay genre as an opportunity to play with language or to experiment with various approaches to rhetoric. For too many, essay writing has become some kind of rote assessment.

If we write along with our students, our appreciation for their academic struggles and triumphs is deeper. Some people might assume that teachers who write outside of their professional responsibilities are better at teaching writing because they have the answers, but it is, paradoxically, the inverse: teacher/writers may be better at teaching writing because we are acutely aware that we do not have all the answers to writing well.

It is this willingness to break patterns, play with language in a variety of ways, and examine the various approaches to how we think about both writing and teaching writing that produces the most positive results.

Many of us were writers before we became teachers, and we will probably be writers long after we have retired from our professional teaching careers. Reflecting on our own writing processes, we realize that we developed and nurtured a luxury of techniques and choices that we make in our work. Our students, unfortunately, don't necessarily feel that they have a host of tools to use or choices they can make. We can provide them those tools.

Outstanding educators and educational theorists have long worked to develop pedagogy and strategies designed to correct the problems we encounter in student written expression. This text offers one plan; however, it is a workable and repeatable one that I have found to be particularly effective with a wide variety of students—coming into the classroom with various levels of academic success—across a number of years of teaching in widely different teaching environments.

Learning how to write effectively and create powerful rhetoric takes time and a great many specific skills, but writing well can be taught. First, however, we have to generate excitement in writing, in the process itself, by encouraging our students to once again (or for the first time) play with language.

What I discovered, almost accidentally at first and then by deliberate design, was that giving students more freedom in deciding how to create their product caused them to become more invested in the work. Teaching them creative techniques and offering various models that could be used to express a concept or a thesis and scaffolding that creative technique instruction has resulted in better student product and students' greater investment of time and effort.

Taking the time to talk with students about their drafts and experiments in one-on-one conferences has proven to be highly effective as well, as many educators, including Nancy Atwell, have demonstrated in studies and practice. But before a student is willing to do the hard work of creating multiple drafts, he or she must feel invested in the ideas and the product.

If your students are already writing powerful, riveting, and flawless essays and compositions, keep doing exactly what you are doing because it must be right. However, if you and your students are not pleased with the results of their written products, try the researched, creative approaches outlined in this text. Indirectly, students had a great deal to do with designing this methodology. Their comments, evaluations, and self-reflective writing compositions pointed to this creative approach and their greater successes.

The student writing samples in *Breaking Open the Box* offer evidence of how creative choice and an infusion of creative techniques may elevate writing. In addition, the application of creative techniques also generates critical thinking. In order to use the techniques, students must revisit the texts and their own writing, and it is through this recursive process that new ways of examining ideas or analyzing texts are born.

The sample compositions are not included to demonstrate that all student products will suddenly be amazing if the students and teachers follow the suggestions outlined here, but these examples of student writing show tremendous creativity, self-selection, few grammatical errors, and results that are intriguing and positive. We have discovered that students become more engaged in their academic writing and reading experiences after experimenting with these techniques.

The thesis behind this text echoes that found in Peter Elbow's text *Writing with Power*, in which he states, "I have found that people produce their best writing when they finally have ideas that are powerful and exciting to them."[1] Students ask better questions in addition to producing better products when they are engaged and take ownership of their academic work. Creative choice, creative frameworks, and creative techniques more readily engage students in the writing process.

Students also begin to read with a trained eye, think critically, and interpret with the knowledge of the skilled writer as well as the reader. Of course, formal academic writing must be taught, but our instruction in writing should allow the writer room to play with language as well as practice it. In "The Modern Essay," Virginia Woolf addressed both the importance of creativity in the essay form and the problems intrinsic in "decorating" the genre a scant eight paragraphs into her argument.

> Yet, if the essay admits more properly than biography or fiction of sudden boldness and metaphor, and can be polished till every atom of its surface shines, there are dangers in that too. We are soon in sight of ornament. Soon the current, which is the life-blood of literature, runs slow; and instead of sparkling and flashing or moving with a quieter impulse which has a deeper excitement, words coagulate together in frozen sprays which, like the grapes on a Christmas-tree, glitter for a single night, but are dusty and garish the day after. The temptation to decorate is great where the theme may be of the slightest.[2]

We need look no further than Woolf's essays, however, to find ample evidence of creativity and "decorative" language in every line. Her arguments are sound and complex, but her language "glitters" for much longer than one night. The artistry—as much as the argument—is why we read her work.

The essay is the type of writing that all students who go on to college must learn to do effectively, but writing well is a lifelong skill required of all citizens in a working democracy, not just those who go to college or professional schools.

The way we teach composition needs revision and daring if we are to engage all of our students and help them in the struggle to become more articulate and think critically about texts and the messages their writing conveys. We owe it to our students and our society to help children think more deeply, in addition to supporting them in their efforts to become better communicators.

The search for the best techniques and the application choices involved in employing creative techniques helps students incorporate more sophisticated processes in both their writing and critical thinking. Instead of following a given template, the students are reading, self-selecting, and thinking deeply about the choices they make and how those decisions will affect their writing.

It may feel like playing with language to them, but it is the real work of scholarship, of learning to understand how language works on readers and how shifts in language, in structure, evoke new meanings. Modeled in the following chapters are creative techniques and student applications of those techniques, demonstrating how thesis statements of argument and instruction can successfully take place within frameworks designed by the student.

In addition, even the design of this text models a creative framework, breaking—in a number of ways—from more traditional instructional texts and demonstrating how we can instruct in other shapes, as shown in writing excerpts within the chapters and the poetry dedication "English Class," found at the conclusion of the book, in which the students personify literary movements.

Creativity and analysis do not need to exist on separate planes. The best essayists show us the same principle through their craft, their work woven out of metaphors, driven by narrative, and argued with metonymy. If employed with a deft touch and opportunities for students to practice and sometimes, as Samuel Beckett wrote in his parodist prose piece *Worstward Ho,* just a few years before he died, "Ever tried. Ever failed. No matter. Try again. Fail again. Fail better,"[3] the methodology outlined here will not only generate positive outcomes for students but will result in a more enjoyable teaching experience for instructors as well.

We have to be as willing to let our students fail and fail better as they begin their journeys to becoming writers, deeper thinkers, and true scholars in the same way that we become better educators.

SUMMARY NOTES

Teachers who enjoy creatively playing with language transmit that love of the language to students. Language play stimulates students' interest in writing and writing process, resulting in improved academic writing and higher levels of engagement.

SECTION 2: TAKING CREATIVE RISKS TO IMPROVE WRITING

We frequently find that students avoid writing—when they are able to do so—and avoid risk taking in writing to try to earn a merely acceptable grade rather than express a concern about just what it is that they are learning or struggling to analyze. Writing well is about taking risks—calculated ones, however. There is an inherent danger involved in concentrating too much on the grade and not the product, as Elbow attests to in the introduction to his text *Writing with Power*:

> Defensive writing means not risking: not risking complicated thoughts or language, not risking half-understood ideas, not risking language that has the resonance that comes from being close to the bone. Students can get rid of badness if they avoid these risks, but they don't have much chance of true excellence unless they take them.[4]

There are many factors both inside a classroom and beyond its walls that impact and influence student product, but we can begin with identifying what negatively affects student writing in the classroom. Specifically, before teachers and college instructors will be willing to incorporate creative techniques in their instructional plans and allow students to play with language and writing, we need to examine the very real concerns that educators may have about creative applications in writing.

- Teachers may have fears about the effect of creative risk taking on test data, increasingly related to job security.
- Teachers, in particular freshman composition instructors, may have concerns that the time element needed to try new techniques and teaching practices is difficult to build into the semester curriculum.
- Teachers may express concerns about effectively evaluating work that they are perhaps not as comfortable with scoring.
- Teachers may be apprehensive about instructing students in creative techniques that they are not accustomed to applying in writing.
- Teachers may recognize that this process will involve rewriting scoring rubrics and will, initially, be time consuming.
- Students may have concerns that their experimentation in writing will result in lower scores, particularly at first.
- Students may recognize that greater time commitment and additional drafts are necessary in order to incorporate the creative techniques into the assignment.
- Students are apt to recognize that the critical thinking involved in writing more creatively involves a greater time investment on assignments.
- Students and teachers may have a fear of letting go of the familiar even when the familiar is not working well.

Educators understand the difficulty of accepting this challenge even while acknowledging that a change is needed if we are to improve student writing and help our students think independently and critically. Too many very well-intentioned educators have made it too easy for students—handing out teacher-constructed outlines, graphic organizers, and fill-in-the-blank "writing" activities—with the consequence being that students are divested of making their own way, avoiding struggling to create their own paths to a more rigorous examination of concepts and the thoughtful articulation of those ideas.

Writer, futurist, and educator Alvin Toffler and Stanford University President John Hennessey have been credited with the words, "The illiterate of the 21st century will not be those who cannot read and write, but those who cannot learn, unlearn and relearn."[5] Allowing our students more creative choice is one way of offering them practice in how to learn and unlearn; how they meet the assignment specifications moves them toward the 21st Century goals of self-direction, decision making that affects outcomes and generates creative, critical thinking.

Of course, learning and unlearning in order to learn anew even sounds arduous and associated with some peril for educators as well as for students. While this movement may initially increase teachers' and students' anxieties, persistence and confidence in the processes will reward all of us.

Students' fears about writing process can be categorized into two areas, primarily: time investment and grade-point concerns. In some respects, high school seniors and college freshmen are the most reluctant to try new approaches to writing assignments because they have come to rely on established, learned patterns even when those patterns have proven to be ineffective.

Getting students to spend more time reading and writing, however, may be one of the most difficult challenges in education at any level. If we can introduce a methodology that causes them to revisit their writing again and again, we will have moved them closer toward scholarship.

There is a profusion of built-in distractions leading away from educational experiences, however. By using some of the technology students love and live with as an entrance to teaching writing, we can adopt one approach that works well, particularly as a "hook" to get them to try something new before the results become the motivator.

Educators are still in control of guiding the lesson and the expected outcomes. Teachers have to see that positive connection between using these techniques and student improvement in writing in order to buy into this methodology. We are continually engaged in reflective practices and professional development that has us adapting to the latest trends in educational theory and practice.

In examining the resistance to trying creative approaches to writing assignments in the classroom, however, we find that sometimes teachers experience more hesitancy to these changes than our students. Just as we ask of our students, we need educators to believe that the risks and time required to make changes to improve writing and critical thinking are worth it.

This is a difficult time in education to be encouraging taking risks, but the willingness to try new ideas is the only way educators are going to break patterns formed in a cultural malaise that has students devaluing the role of education (and reading and writing) in their lives. The Common Core State Standards discussion (see chapter 14) is filled with emphatic statements about how to improve students' education—demanding a greater emphasis on informational and explanatory writing—but students need an entrance to writing first.

The new Common Core also asks us to help students approximate real-world scenarios in the educational processes. It asks us to challenge students and foster their creativity—a perfect fit for the methodology outlined here. Teaching creative techniques and allowing students the freedom to make choices about their writing help students discover that writing a text of any kind or length is worth the time spent to do it well.

It is worth reiterating here that the Common Core conversation centers on the importance of students' abilities to comprehend complex texts; the introduction, application, and support for creative techniques in writing simultaneously foster critically thinking about higher-level texts—resulting in better reading comprehension, due to the increased time spent with the text—and the application of editing and writing processes.

Students who take ownership of their written products and are invested in their work are willing to both think profoundly about texts and work at revisions that produce writing that more closely approximates the complexity of their thoughts.

Considering the concepts of taking risks and the willingness to support the risk taker, educator Bruce Pirie stated:

> The challenge is to find other ways of writing about ideas and meanings. We need forms of exposition that don't force students to pose as individual authorities, but rather encourage tentative and cooperative exploration. We need to relax the pressure to encapsulate thought in a thesis and develop instead forms that invite divergent thinking, value opposing ideas, and make it possible to examine complex processes and forge meaningful links.[6]

Allowing our students to have more freedom in making choices about formats and vehicles for their ideas expressed on the page helps guide them to the desired results: better articulation of sophisticated thoughts, self-direction, and critical thinking.

SUMMARY NOTES

We have to confront our own fears about risk taking and test scores before we can expect to help our students learn to write rhetoric with power and voice.

3

Recognizing the Problem

SECTION 1: A FAMILIAR SCENE

Teacher 1: The results are in, and the verdict is—

Teacher 2: (gestures indicating exasperation) Really bad writing.

Teacher 1: (sighing) Well, not all of it. Let's focus on the best for a moment. What was the best student essay you have ever read?

Teacher 2: The one I just read was only slightly ridiculous. I'm still trying to figure out what my student intended.

Teacher 1: I know you can recall an excellent one. Try again. The best. Why was it memorable? Why was it effective?

Teacher 2: (pensive for a moment) It contained a dialogue within the essay. It was clever and insightful, but that kind of writing is rare.

Teacher 1: So there are not a lot of remarkable student essays?

Teacher 2: (laughing) Not really.

Teacher 1: Why not? What do we typically get from our students?

Teacher 2: Too often, we get hollow containers, inane or even illogical writing.

Teacher 1: What do we want from our students' writing?

Teacher 2: We want our students to write penetrating, original, convincing, and effective arguments with sophisticated style and distinctive voice, but there are very few like that. Admittedly, that is a very difficult task.

Teacher 1: Where do you think the solution lies? Why are we getting such poor quality work from our students when we work so hard to provide them with the structure, tools, and techniques?

Teacher 2: Maybe we're doing too much. Do our students feel invested in their work? I don't think they do. We get summary, repetition, and unconvincing, unappealing student writing. We have provided the container—the five-paragraph essay—and require our students to fill it rather than ask that they choose a vessel to fit their ideas.

Teacher 1: Writing is harder than it looks. It's never simple, is it?

Teacher 2: Maybe we could try something different once again? We are willing. We are always interested in trying something new if it will help them.

Teacher 1: During my first year of teaching, I learned something about process. After handing back their essays, I told my students, "This is the best writing you've done this year and the first time I was not breathing down your necks."

Teacher 2: What are you suggesting?

Teacher 1: That we give them more creative choices, that we empower them to make more of their own decisions in the writing process; that we do less for them, allowing them to become part of the teaching/writing process.

Teacher 2: (hesitantly at first, but then resolutely) I'll try anything if it will help my students become better writers.

Modeling a creative approach in presenting an argument via dialogue, here we have an atypical way of examining the problem with student writing. We must, however, admit that the first step in improving student writing may be to recognize how difficult it is to write well. We need to allow our students to make "mistakes," try approaches that may or may not be effective; in other words, they need to experiment to learn from their writing experiences.

From another perspective, as sports columnist Walter Wellesley "Red" Smith wrote, "There's nothing to writing. All you do is sit down at a typewriter and open a vein."[1] Picking up a pen or sitting at a keyboard is the only easy part of the process.

In identifying exactly what we want for our students, we can agree that some of our instruction is actually counterproductive, yet we all have the same goals. We want our students to

- be thoughtfully engaged in learning;
- think deeply about and critically analyze texts;
- read and write across a wide spectrum;
- make connections to prior learning and subject areas;
- progressively build writing skills;
- write with awareness of audience and purpose;

- write with distinctive and original style;
- formulate questions about readings and concepts to be expressed in writing;
- be enriched by writing;
- be empowered by reading and writing well; and
- be successful communicators in the wider world.

It is possible for us to promote this type of thinking in our students and teach them to improve their writing if we are willing to delve into the same processes that writers use: experiment or play with style, form, function, and techniques.

SUMMARY NOTES

Writing well is admittedly difficult, but our instruction in writing needs to change if we expect better results from our students.

SECTION 2: WHY THE ESSAY GENRE PRESENTS SUCH CHALLENGES

Where do we begin? Elementary school teachers frequently include creative writing applications in their lessons, but as students move into secondary school, the shift away from the creative and personal to the analytical is dramatic, even severe. High school teachers do have to prepare students for the rigors of academic writing in secondary school and college, but we also need to bring the creative into that realm more effectively.

"Students, please write a five-paragraph essay."
"Write an essay describing your personal health regimen."
"Compose an essay in which you discuss Chinua Achebe's critique of Conrad's racism as revealed in *Heart of Darkness*."
"Compose a 500-word essay in which you narrate your life story in a way that divulges all of the reasons why a college should choose you over every other applicant."
"Compose a one-paragraph classification essay."

The essay genre in all its permutations is much more varied and difficult for our students than we would like to admit. The more essays students are exposed to, the more uncertain they become about the genre and how to navigate within it or produce coherent works in the genre.

Students write essays from elementary school through high school and beyond. Why is the task of writing a good essay so difficult and the answer to our quandary so evasive? Clear delineation of the essay genre is slippery even for professional educators and writers (many of whom are engaged in the current debate over the position of the lyric essay).

English teachers provide models and definitions for analytic, evaluation, speculative, argumentative, definition, descriptive, expository, comparison/contrast, division/classification, personal narrative, research, and cause-and-effect essays, and this list goes on and on. The dictionary definition states that essays are a "short" literary composition, yet Henry David Thoreau's "Civil Disobedience" is often classified as an essay, and the 1849 political work is by no means a "short composition."

It actually gets harder for our students to write a good essay the more they are exposed to the essay. They grapple with genre identification even as they struggle to encapsulate a moment in their lives in order to meet academic requirements.

In a 2002 issue of *Poets & Writers*, Michael Depp addressed the genre's difficulty:

> This is not an essay. Though maybe, in a way, it is. Because it's a strange thing about essays—even talking about them, trying to get at what they are, it's hard to cleave to the spirit of the essay, that inconclusive, most outwardly formless of forms, which spills and seeps into so many other kinds of writing—memoir, feature, commentary, review—and punctuates every assertion with a qualification, a measure of doubt, an alternate possibility.[2]

Reading Depp's commentary, we may think about Virginia Woolf and her brilliant feminist polemic *A Room of One's Own*, in which she employs a fictional narrative in relating the story of one Judith Shakespeare, William's talented but ultimately suicidal sister. It is a surprise to students to find that techniques employed in fiction may also be employed by writers of the essay form. English teachers are well aware that many of the great essayists dip into that region typically reserved for fiction writers, using narrative when it helps to make a point or strengthen the rhetoric.

Yet using narrative is only one of the many creative options open to essayists. Ralph Waldo Emerson's classic essay "Self-Reliance" begins with a poem, an epilogue by another poet. Jonathan Swift's essay "A Modest Proposal" suggests that the British eat Irish children in the most bitingly satirical piece of writing ever produced, without once succumbing to apology. Edgar Allan Poe begins his essay "American Poetry" with a deliberate contradiction and double negative.

How do young writers learn to extend their definition of the essay into this myriad of transmutations and still recognize the genre? Where does a musing leave off and an essay begin? Stephen Jay Gould's work in the book *The Flamingo's Smile: Reflections in Natural History* has been written about extensively as a collection of "thirty essays" or reflection essays.

David Mamet's "Secret Names," from *The Best American Nonrequired Reading*, begins in a musing—"We Americans love nicknames and acronyms"—and ends in a polemic on the powerful and political nature of naming such policing actions as "Homeland Security," comparing the nomenclature to a European construct, specifically, *die Heimat*, or motherland of Germany during Nazi rule.[3] At the end of Mamet's piece, there can no longer be any doubt that we have just read an essay, nor is there doubt that students will feel they have walked into unfamiliar rooms.

In examining models of the genre, we find these writers breaking many of the rules that we teach our students. The thesis statements of these great writers do not appear in the introductory paragraph; in fact, the thesis may not even be explicit. We certainly don't see a thesis in the first paragraph of Mamet's essay or in the first pages of Woolf's argument. In fact, in the best writing, the thesis may be implied rather than overtly stated, and it is seldom the first sentence or even in the introduction.

Part of the difficulty is that teachers feel the need to simplify classifications to help students wrap their minds around difficult concepts, but simplifying a genre and providing the "building blocks" may eventually make that "thing" unrecognizable to less experienced readers and writers. Not wanting to permanently scare off our students, we avoid telling them that they are about to write an exegesis rather than a literary analysis of the allusions to Job in a particular work of literature.

Yet we want them to understand that Salman Rushdie essays that contain narrative are still, in fact, essays and not short stories. Although well-known as a novelist, Rushdie's essays—like Woolf's—are the richer because he incorporates narrative within his rhetoric.

Teaching involves bringing our students through an initiation process of learning not just to write but also to write well. As experienced readers, we know that powerful writing moves seamlessly between some of the arbitrary distinctions we make for students who are treading water in the early stages of their development as writers. After we teach them the five-paragraph essay structure, how long is it before we let our students know that the best writers dive in and out of the delineations within the genre like loons on a deep-water lake?

With outstanding writers, we find that the structure is dictated by the content, not the other way around. Peter Elbow suggests minimizing the distinction between creative writing and expository writing in *Writing with Power*:

> What is usually called "creative writing"—poems, stories, novels—feels very different to most people from what is usually called "nonfiction" or "expository writing"—essays, reports, memos, biography, and so on. . . . I want to underline the fact that a good essay or biography requires just

> as much creativity as a good poem; and that a good poem requires just as much truth as a good essay.[4]

We can teach students to analyze something as complex as Chinua Achebe's critique of Joseph Conrad's bias expressed through his diction in *Heart of Darkness* without abandoning creativity. In fact, understanding and applying poetic techniques in writing and making creative choices about style and structure will help students discover new ways in which to analyze both Conrad's and Achebe's divergent perspectives on colonialism and imperialism, race and culture.

SECTION 3: THE HOLLOW MIDDLE

Emphasis on form and structure seems to result too often in a vacuous or nearly incomprehensible piece of writing. Bruce Pirie wrote of the five-paragraph essay in his text *Reshaping High School English*:

> In our own time, the formulaic five-paragraph essay has been justified as a necessary first step for immature writers. . . . On the one hand, it makes structure all-important, because students will be judged on how well they have mastered the form. On the other hand, it implies that structure can't be very important: it clearly doesn't have any inherent relationship to ideas since just about any idea can be stuffed into the same form.[5]

Traditionally, we have provided our students with instruction relating to the structure without necessarily conceding that choosing the form is integral to the content as well as the value.

If we support students taking creative risks with writing in the classroom, the results will surprise us. Their attempts with creative language play and unusual structures or frameworks for their writing may also frighten us. An intriguing discovery—made while allowing students to have greater freedom in creatively interpreting writing assignments—is that some of the students who produced mundane or unclear essays were the first to blossom when permitted to use more creative approaches to the writing task.

Educator and author Robyn R. Jackson offers this advice: "Share with students the goal of the lesson and give students several choices as to how they can meet that goal."[6] *Choice* is the key word here if we want our students to become more engaged. Choice also involves critical thinking, as students must consider and weigh the advantages or disadvantages of various options. Jackson also suggests that we "discuss with students the pros and cons of each approach so that students can make intelligent decisions."[7] We should guide students in this process while still allowing them to make these decisions.

Young writers need good models and time in a classroom to analyze these models and experiments with writing and critical thinking. They also need a safety net when they stumble on their new high-wire acts. After providing students with examples of various creative approaches to the essay, a number of students will still be resistant to experiment with form.

Initially, many refuse to venture away from the strictures of the traditional essay format and style. In my writing workshops, there is no penalty for non-experimentation but neither is there a grade penalty for trying a new approach—even when the approach is not particularly successful.

The grade should be based on the specific criteria the teacher has previously outlined in a rubric and shared with students. Over time, however, we discover that every student is eventually willing to experiment with their creative choices in writing even if those choices involve only diction and not the framework.

One Advanced Placement (AP) English Literature and Composition student stayed within the traditional structure of the analytical essay the entire semester until the very last assignment. He was so excited about his experiment, however, that he sought out his teacher to discuss his writing project after school hours. Without asking for the grade on the paper, he knew it was his best work of the year and a project he would remember for a long time to come. The transcendent aspect is that he was most excited about the ideas that the risk taking in his writing had generated.

By allowing students to choose the time and assignment for their experiments in creative approaches to writing tasks, you automatically build in differentiation but some additional work for teachers. Blocking time for discussion about the successes and "missteps" in their experiments in writing is a key strategy to helping students analyze what works and what was unwieldy in dealing with their task applications.

There is not one creative approach in writing that works with every student, but allowing students to decide on certain aspects of the writing task has the potential to greatly improve their writing and level of engagement in the lessons. Aligned with 21st Century learning goals, the Common Core, and the new National Standards, the creative approach and introduction of creative techniques to academic writing assignments increase the role that students play in their own education, giving them considerable responsibility and engrossing them in their own processes as well as products.

A contract is implied here, however. If a student attempts to try an experimental approach to a writing task, that student and teacher should discuss the approach and how the lesson's essential questions will be explored through the writing. It also suggests that the teacher give the student a degree of latitude and not unduly "punish" the student, in terms of the grade, for an approach that did not fully meet the intended result. A well-designed lesson plan with essential questions, goals, and rubric should allow for some flexibility in how the writing goals are met.

SECTION 4: WHEN A GOOD STUDENT WRITES A BAD ESSAY

> It takes time to write well, time to develop ideas, time to edit, and time to revise product.

How many times in a classroom have we seen intelligent students make ridiculous or even incoherent statements in writing? "People often sound dumber and more incoherent on paper than they really are," states Peter Elbow in his text *Writing with Power*.[8] My students would subscribe to this theory. We see the frustration on their faces when they attempt to give both oral and written coherency to the sophisticated thoughts that are being formulated. "Well, I know what it's about. I understand it; it's just—"

Students will frequently create elaborate stories to explain why they were unable to complete the assignment as outlined in the task. When reduced to honesty, however, most will admit that they simply did not spend enough time on the writing. Time investment is something we can recognize, appreciate, and do something about if we are willing.

In considering students' time expenditure on a project, we should think first about how much time we are willing to spend on professional tasks. If we believe the task is worth the outcome, we will find the time and rearrange our schedule to meet the demands. Conversely, if we find that the task is not particularly valuable, then we are likely to find ways to get around the expectations.

Students do the same. We have to first help them see that the investment of their time in a written product is worth the rescheduling of their other activities. The best way to tackle this challenge is to tie the assignment to something to which the student feels personally invested or allow the student to create the connection through structure or techniques.

From class discussions, we know that many of our students are smart with capable intellects and academic curiosity. A fair number in every class are hard workers, but their written products do not accurately reflect the sophistication of their thinking nor does much of their writing engage them or their readers.

To put it bluntly, student products are often repetitive, confusing, and superficial, to say nothing of the grammatical and mechanical errors with which their writing is frequently plagued. More concerning, however, is the incoherency of their written products. Of course, educators try numerous strategies and offer models of good writing and mini-lessons in grammar, mechanics, and style, but students' written results are, typically and surprisingly, unaffected by instruction.

It is not that students are entirely resistant to efforts to teach them, but they often seem unwilling to do anything that suggests a change in entrenched patterns even when those patterns put them at academic risk. These observations appear to be shared across the curricula and across educational environments. The weak, inarticulate writing we find in many of our students' examples of writing is not confined to English classrooms. It seems that everything we read by educators addresses this frustration with students' writing.

After reading student surveys about writing, I found that they felt constricted by all of the rules to the point that they had begun to hate any kind of writing. Writing was no longer about expression but, to quote them, "torture." To many students, writing defines their *lack*, the response suggesting a well-meaning institutional structure that has managed to exclude rather than include.

David Bartholomae, in recognizing the problems that students face in attempting to write well, stated, "Literacy . . . requires the ability to work within and against the languages of a closed, privileged discourse."[9] It has become obvious to many educators that far too many of our students feel like aliens within this discourse.

Our students need both an entrance to the codes of that privileged language and more freedom to make both creative and analytical choices about how to use those codes for various rhetorical purposes. More choices must belong to the student rather than to the teacher. This, of course, involves educators giving up some control.

What happens too often when no creative risks are taken in the classroom? A few examples of student writing shown in this book provide illustrations of the types of mistakes and lack of clarity that normally good academic students sometimes make in their writing when they do not feel invested in the product. In addition to problems with grammar and mechanics, however, is the much more distressing evidence—found in students' writing—of a lack of logic and meaning.

We all have experienced reading student work that implies a number of complex ideas, but where the student struggles to state exactly what is intended. Smart students often use fairly sophisticated vocabulary inaccurately, resulting in lack of clarity. Modification errors, such as "the story is able to related to a vast group of people because they can adapt the setting," and other grammatical errors further reduce the clarity and cohesion of the intended arguments. In other words, intelligent students with good academic records still may have significant and serious problems with writing.

In reading their passages aloud during the teacher/writer conferencing process, each student winced at his or her own words and constructions. They knew that the writing made little sense, yet they were perfectly ready to hand in the work after the initial draft. Why?

If these struggles sound familiar, you will join the teachers already scratching their heads, grimacing, or trying not to yell or cry because we care about our students and we believe in them. Whatever grade level or course we teach, we will receive composition papers and essays with lapses in precision, diction, grammar, and mechanics from our students, but most seriously, we recognize their failure to successfully convey meaning in writing.

Ironically, it seems that the higher level of education students are exposed to, the greater the risk of written incoherency. Second graders rarely construct a sentence devoid of meaning because that child's sentence is typically straightforward, consisting of one noun and one verb with few other words in the sentence. Modifiers, parenthetical phrasing, gerunds, participle phrases, and subordination come later, and with them come sentence and language function complications that have a tendency to wrap around our students' intended meanings like little snakes and strangle clarity.

What is required here is editing coupled with the willingness to revise. These tasks can be fun and engaging if the student has a stake in the product. If not, then the tasks of editing and revision are too often ignored.

If we ask our students why they think their essays and compositions are unsuccessful, they are often honest and direct—after their initial attempts to cover for themselves:

- I didn't know what to write.
- I didn't get it.
- I didn't care about the assignment. What's the point?
- I didn't spend any time on it. I had a game last night.
- It was boring.
- I couldn't explain it, but I understand it. Maybe I don't understand it.

Educational theorists will state that writing is a recursive process, meaning that we have to move back in order to move forward, or, stated another way, we need to revisit what we have written and edited before returning to the beginning as we once again proceed to an ending. It is in this recursive process that our thinking becomes more defined and our writing becomes lucid.

If, however, students are not taking the time to move back and forth in their compositions, in the writing process, returning again and again to examine their words and structures, refining, editing, revising, they will find that their writing lacks the power of their thinking.

Yet here again a dilemma occurs, as neatly identified by Elbow: "When we put ourselves in a correcting, fault-finding frame of mind, we usually have more trouble coming up with new and interesting ideas."[10] Furthermore, we know that the processes of editing and creating new ideas are time consuming. If students are not deeply engaged in the work they are doing, they are unwilling to spend the time needed to allow these processes to take place and make room for successful, intriguing writing and rhetoric.

How do we best engage our students in the process of learning and writing? In her article in the *ASCD Journal*, titled "Springing into Active Learning," education consultant Alison Zmuda wrote:

> For students to move beyond lip-syncing someone else's words, ideas, and solutions, they need the opportunity to struggle with a task that inspires their performance, that motivates them to do more than just go through the motions of learning and truly understand what the discipline requires. Just because students write a thousand paragraphs in middle school does not mean they are becoming writers or can even articulate what a paragraph is.[11]

Clearly, writing a lot or simply practicing writing drills is not going to produce better student writing unless something else takes place. Writing instruction is about much more than assigning writing. The students, unfortunately, are not the only ones facing barriers to writing well.

SUMMARY NOTES

Our students need both an entrance to the codes of academic, privileged language and more freedom to make both creative and analytical choices about how to use those codes for various rhetorical purposes.

SECTION 5: WHEN A STUDENT SURPRISES WITH HIS OR HER WRITING

Teachers may recognize the experience of suddenly coming across a wonderful composition by a weak academic student who almost inexplicably writes something that pulls us in and evokes both emotion and thought. How does this happen? Elbow writes metaphorically in *Writing with Power* about this familiar scenario:

> When writing is really good on the other hand, the words themselves lend some of their own energy to the writer. The writer is controlling words which he can't turn his back on without the danger of being scratched or bitten. . . . This explains why it is sometimes easier for a blocked and incoherent

> writer to break into powerful language than for someone who is fluent and verbal and can always write just what he wants. . . . It will take this obedient writer much longer to get power.[12]

Many of us will recall such moments when grading a group of poems. To share one anecdote, I remember one creative writing class in which I came to the haiku of a student who had been classified with an individualized educational plan (IEP). I read the poem and reread it, struck by the beauty and effectiveness of his words. Although this student had struggled greatly with essay writing and organizing his ideas in compositions in other classes, his poetry had an intensity, beauty, and precision that so many of the other students' poems lacked:

> Dancing leaves on trees
> Frozen in the essence: time
> set free

This student continued to write wonderful, original poetry, so it was not simply one application of words but his creative energy behind them that was so dynamic. When presented with just one boundary and prompt to inspire the poem—that of incorporating a description of a painting in a poem—this student's work showed intelligence and poetic artistry as well as great skill with language. As an endnote to the anecdote related here, this student went on to community college and worked to form a writing group while there.

> **As Told by Brueghel**
> As told by Brueghel,
> Before Icarus fell,
> He flew up to the sun
>
> Bright silver wings glowing,
> Melting them in the midst of his triumph
> He plummeted into the sea
>
> Joyous children playing
> People laughing
> Singing
>
> The sea was still with each passing moment
> Icarus gasping to his father
>
> Then . . . silence
> No gleam of hope.
> Nothing.

This student's work demonstrates the potential of children that can be found through metaphoric language. This young man took a greater interest in his writing following the class in which he began to write poetry. Without question, writing creatively empowered him in an arena in which he had often felt very little power or sense of academic growth. Why not bring these elements into all of our classrooms?

Creative techniques and their application are causal to divergent thinking. They also offer "another way writers get physical."[13] And this physicality allows entrance to students who see much of the world through tactile means.

SUMMARY NOTES

Creative approaches and creative techniques allow entrance into academic writing, scholarship, and—most important—self-expression for students who may appear to struggle academically.

4

Outlining Creative Applications to Academic Writing

SECTION 1: WHERE TO START AND HOW TO PROCEED WITH INSTRUCTION IN CREATIVE TECHNIQUES AND CREATIVE CHOICES

How does a teacher introduce creative approaches and creative techniques into his or her classroom? This chapter provides a starting point and offers sample writing assignments with instructional goals and student writing that demonstrates how the students responded to assignments as well as met the lesson objectives. The assessment rubrics and discussion of how the assignment meets the new Common Core State Standards will be elaborated on in chapters 14 and 15. The student works included in this chapter may also be used as models for other students seeking to try a different approach to argument and analysis.

The courses from which these student paper excerpts were drawn include Advanced Placement (AP) English Literature and Composition, Creative Writing I and II, College Prep English, and the college comp course English 099. The range of students enrolled in these courses offers a wide spectrum of the population and diversity, from students at the top of a class to those who have recently been mainstreamed into general education courses. Although the examples include both high school and college student writing in response to a wide variety of topics and level of assignments, these selections show the application of creative techniques and creative choice that could be applied by students at any level. How the writing meets the instructional goals is indicated with the task and lesson objectives.

Starting with Metaphors

After reviewing students' answers to a Creative Writing course survey, I was surprised to find that so many students identified learning how to use metaphors as the reason that their writing improved. There is a vast difference between "knowing" a definition and being able to use the concept behind a word in writing. By supplying our students with these tools, we engender innovation as well as entrance to thinking and to writing—a compelling gift. Writers know this almost instinctively, but it is time to pass on this knowledge through deliberate instruction.

Novelist and short story writer Annie Proulx wrote about the necessity of this pursuit of metaphors in the second paragraph of her article "Inspiration? Head Down the Back Road, and Stop for the Yard Sales," which appeared in *The New York Times*:

> A whole set of metaphoric shovels is part of my tool collection, and for me the research that underlies the writing is the best part of the scribbling game. Years ago, alder scratched, tired, hungry, and on a late return from a fishing trip, I was driving through Maine when a hubbub on the sidewalk caught my eye: milling customers at a yard sale. I stop for yard sales.[1]

Why the Metaphor?

Our yard sale begins with instruction in metaphors and their application. A teacher using this text as a guide could start introducing any technique into the writing instruction, but we start with direct instruction and practice creating metaphors for a number of reasons. Students' ability to comprehend metaphors instantly improves not only their writing but their reading of texts, generating deeper levels of thinking about language and how language simultaneously operates on various levels. Metaphor creation generates divergent thinking and offers an array of associations that take the reader in various directions simultaneously.

While this is a text designed to improve students' writing, the improvement in their reading level is equally important to them (and strengthens their writing, too). Metaphors are a great technique to start with because they can be easily grasped with simple applications, and the level of sophistication can be scaffolded in assignments that increase in difficulty with the age and level of ability of the students. Creating metaphors in order to express an idea (and, later, an argument in an essay) also aligns neatly with the Common Core State Standard related to Knowledge of Language:

1. Apply knowledge of language to understand how language functions in different contexts, to make effective choices for meaning or style, and to comprehend more fully when reading or listening.

In addition, the practice of writing with metaphors meets another of the Common Core State Standards:

> Demonstrate understanding of figurative language, word relationships, and nuances in word meanings.
> a. Interpret figures of speech (e.g., hyperbole, paradox) in context and analyze their role in the text
> b. Analyze nuances in the meaning of words with similar denotations.

The use of metaphors actually changes how we think about language as well as the concepts behind the metaphoric expression.

Metaphors Aimed at Meeting Twenty-First Century Skills and Bloom's Taxonomy

Guiding students through the processes of creating metaphoric language also meets the highest levels of skill development on Bloom's Taxonomy, as shown in the language from the document: "creativity involves skills of flexibility, originality, elaboration, modification, imagery, attribute listing, and metaphorical thinking."[2] In addition, the 21st Century Skills Framework lists "creativity and innovation" as top priorities for our students' development as writers and critical thinkers. Active research has shown that direct instruction in use of metaphors has a positive and immediate effect on improving student writing. The importance of this creative technique and creative choice instruction is clear and has been articulated for educators by the new frameworks set out for us.

Yet another reason to begin with metaphor direct instruction is because it offers the potential for fun, and language play creates enjoyment for the writer. We know that if we enjoy the task, we are more likely to spend time working it at, improving it, revising it—in other words, the writing process. These discussions and writing practice could range from an examination of the language play in Dr. Seuss books to Shakespeare's puns and double entendres in *Hamlet*.

Instruction in, as well as practice in, using metaphors has such a profound effect on improving students' writing and reading comprehension, as stated previously. Using metaphors works to improve student writing in a ninth-grade high school class as well as in a freshman comp course. I have successfully used these creative techniques with students who were mainstreamed into a general education classroom for the first time and with the brightest students in AP English Literature and Composition. Of course, the final products are not equal, but the baseline and post-instruction written product results show dramatic improvement for all students using this creative technique. The beauty of the strategy is that it may be incorporated in a writing workshop, direct instruction, or group instruction. How the strategy is fused into the individual teacher's lesson plan is decided by that teacher.

After we write our metaphoric "experiments," we discuss how the technique changes meaning, allowing us to think about the topics in differing ways. Follow-up with individual, group, or workshop discussion is integral to writing improvement as well. Students need the opportunity to discuss what worked and what was less than successful in their writing applications.

SECTION 2: APPLICATIONS WITH METAPHOR

If asked what a metaphor is, nearly every high school student can repeat a definition. If asked, however, to create a metaphor, students stutter, and then they appear puzzled. It seems that applying techniques allows students to incorporate the concept of the technique in a way that memorization of definitions will never allow. Introducing metaphors is good starting point for improving student writing and critical thinking about texts because so many texts contain these examples of the "advanced guard of the mind,"[3] as poet Mark Doty expressed so lyrically.

Metaphors work very well to capture the fears and frustrations we feel when we struggle with writing. In fact, metaphor use has been linked to thought processes as well as providing connections to emotion. Educator David Jauss wrote in his article "Who's Afraid of the Big Bad Abstraction?," "The principal advantage of using metaphor and/or body language in conjunction with an abstraction is to make the abstract idea become something we can feel—to make the word become flesh."[4] Students need to feel the words before they can absorb the abstract meanings they convey, and metaphors help them to do that.

Before students can learn to write well, they need to be able to read with comprehension, but too often the text presents such challenges that the child is stalled in making progress. Paradoxically, writing can also be an entrance to reading with better comprehension. Using the metaphor, students gain a sense of power and control, and as Jauss states, "metaphor can particularize an abstraction,"[5] and abstractions present the frozen plain threatening many students' attempts at comprehension.

Students' fears and frustrations are the monster or, in this metaphor, the lion in the room: "As the work grows, it gets harder to control; it is a lion growing in strength. You must visit it every day and reassert your mastery over it. If you skip a day, you are quite rightly afraid to open the door to its room," wrote Annie Dillard in her book of essays *The Writing Life*.[6] In addition to addressing the fears that go along with struggling to identify ourselves as writers, Dillard zeroes in on one of the best remedies for controlling this reluctance—writing every day.

We can teach our students to write their way out of that paralyzing emotion that causes resistance to writing. So writing every day in every class is part of the solution. Dillard's conceit also focuses our attention on another key to solving the dilemma of the reluctant writer: using metaphoric language to creatively express our ideas. In fact, it is impossible to read Dillard or other professional writers without wading deeply in metaphoric language.

Our students need to become more comfortable with reading, interpreting, and employing metaphoric language. Much of the richness of difficult texts lies below the literal or surface levels, and students walking around on the literal are likely to miss multiple layers of meaning. The initial problem is that too often students are intimidated not only by writing but by indirect language. Understanding metaphors is about much more than simply identifying a technique. Metaphors take us to the subtext, the substrata where the meaning lives and changes its skin. Knowing how to use this poetic technique provides an entrance not only to writing and identity but to reading at the inferential, deeper levels intended by authors.

Metaphoric experience becomes practice with critical thinking. Learning how to employ poetic techniques for a desired effect requires a much higher level of skill and is more useful than memorizing definitions for these techniques. After creating their own metaphors and working with inferential language in their writing, students are able to find examples of this comparative language in other texts much more easily. It would seem that part of our difficulty with learning to write well involves how we think, and teaching students how to think in terms of metaphors bolsters their confidence both as readers and writers.

Teaching students to use the full richness of metaphoric language is not easy, however, because it involves a different way of thinking. Peter Elbow underlines this difficulty in the introduction to his text *Writing with Power*: "The germ event in writing—perhaps in thinking itself—is being able to make the move between a piece of nonverbal felt meaning and a piece of language."[7] Too often, high school teachers and professors make the assumption that this jump from thinking to writing can be made seamlessly and naturally before recognizing just how hard this process really is. Elbow states, "Writing itself is unnatural for humans (unlike speaking), and most people avoid it when they can, yet that is not an argument against writing."[8]

We need to help our students bridge the gap between thought and writing down the ideas, and we need to support their risk taking—their trapeze acts—if they are to make the transition into good writers with some degree of grace.

Using Metaphors to Express Concepts about Metaphor: A Simple Exercise

This relatively simple writing exercise involves requiring students to consider the metaphor and write about their ideas of the metaphor by using metaphors. The writing assignment could be incorporated in a daily journal entry (with the prompt) or with a very sophisticated response to literature (as shown with an AP English student's response in this text). I have used this prompt involving metaphor creation in both college and high school classes.

Assignment: Describe what a metaphor means to you by creating a metaphor or metaphors to define and shape your ideas. Your response may take the form of either poetry or prose.

Objectives: Critical thinking about language, comprehension of nuances created by metaphors, expanding meanings through language play

Graduating in complexity, the next assignment asked AP English students to read Mark Doty's ideas about metaphors, read his poem "A Display of Mackerel," and then write a musing or short essay about how the concept of metaphor worked in the creation of ideas. The objective of the assignment was to write a piece that would provoke thought in others and challenge ideas about how a technique shapes or is shaped by thought. Although the following sample could easily be classified as a musing on the topic of metaphor, James's* work addresses both the power and versatility of the metaphor. It is also wonderfully metaphoric!

Assignment: After reading and considering Mark Doty's piece on metaphors, write an original musing, short essay, or vehicle of your choice in which you consider the metaphor and how it works on our thinking. Use at least two metaphors in your written work. You might try a conceit (extended metaphor).

Objectives:

- Develop metaphor comprehension and application.
- Play with language in creative and original ways.
- Express divergent thinking.
- Express critical thinking about the link between metaphor and higher levels of thought processes.
- Incorporate a creative technique in writing that expresses an idea or argument.

James
Metaphor: A Very Handy Tool
A metaphor is both a gateway to a mansion and, at the same time, a rocket to the moon. How is this possible? A metaphor is a comparison so strong

that the two subjects being compared are interpreted as the same entity. Obviously, a metaphor is not literally a rocket to the moon, but the comparisons between the two are striking. The metaphor "he is a rock" can be used to convey an explanation of this seemingly paradoxical statement about a metaphor. A poet writing "he is a rock" does not mean that "he" is literally a "rock" but rather that the poet is commenting on the character or nature of this person; the poet is suggesting that this person is strong, resolute, unwavering, and possibly emotionless. A metaphor does something mere descriptions fail to accomplish. This hypothetical poet could have written out all of these adjectives, but the metaphor succeeded in capturing all that he desired to express. This is the power of the metaphor. Just like a rocket takes a person to the moon, a metaphor can blast a reader to a new level of understanding.

Metaphors are also Swiss Army knives. A writer will use them to accomplish a variety of ends. In Mark Doty's poem "A Display of Mackerel," the poet uses a very well-developed metaphor called a conceit. A conceit is a metaphor that is all grown up. In his poem, there are two major conceits. One of the conceits is between mackerels and humans while the other conceit is between mackerels and art. The conceit between the mackerels and the humans is absolutely essential to understanding Doty's message. The poet asks us to consider mackerels and applies a lesson that is learned from them to humans. Without his conceit, the poem would fall to pieces, a grand mosaic that had not been glued together. Doty's poem, as it currently exists, is completely reliant on this underlying metaphor. His motif of the mackerel's gleaming receives its poetic meaning from the implications it has on humans. In this case, a metaphor was not just a pathway to a simple explanation but a vital knife to a mountain climber who faced the possibility of being stranded on the summit.

A sophisticated writer could get even more skilled in the use of the Swiss Army knife. Juxtaposition is one advanced technique that a writer can utilize to make a reader truly ponder the point that he or she makes. An extreme example of a metaphor that accomplishes juxtaposition is "Hitler is a flower." Hitler, in the league of the most evil men who ever lived, is being compared to a flower, a clichéd symbol of innocence and happiness. Without a doubt, most readers would stop and try to comprehend this statement which does not seem to make sense. The metaphor has accomplished exactly what the author desired; the reader will think about his or her message.

The beauty in a metaphor is that it drastically expands the capacity of our language. Instead of being bound to adjectives, a comparison can be made that incorporates people, places, ideas, or even everyday objects. While a metaphor may not seem to make sense at first, meaning can always be derived by careful analysis. A language without metaphors is a language without one of the most useful and versatile literary devices mankind has developed. Without metaphors, writers could metaphorically be trapped on the summit of Mount Everest without an ever essential Swiss Army knife.

It is unlikely that James will ever again read a passage in any text without being conscious of metaphors and how their use by an author changes meaning, offering various other streams down which to navigate a new course. The exercises with metaphor will take many different shapes, depending on the classroom level and experience. The important points to remember in this type of instruction are that teachers provide good examples of metaphors, discuss how the metaphors cause other levels of thinking about a topic, and then provide opportunities for students to experiment with the technique before more formal, summative assessments take place.

Metaphor and Poetry Practice with Divergent Thinking

As soon as the metaphor is introduced, it is not much of a leap to move into poetry. Teachers may use a number of quotations from poets, historians, and authors in which poetry is defined through metaphor to begin instruction. Instructors might also ask students to find their favorite quotations in which metaphor is used to define a concept. A few favorites:

- "The poet is the priest of the invisible" by Wallace Stevens
- "Poetry is an echo, asking a shadow to dance" by Carl Sandburg
- "What is a poem? . . . Crows punctuating a field of snow" by Jane Yolen
- "Poetry is nearer to vital truth than history" by Plato

While some teachers may feel that the time spent teaching how to create metaphors and poetry could be better spent on test preparation, it can be argued that teaching creative writing and creative techniques is excellent test preparation as well as writing instruction. It was students who taught me that it is through the act of creating their own metaphors that they arrive more quickly at comprehension of meaning found in the complexity of layered texts. When they have created poems and metaphoric expression, students are far more likely to correctly interpret reading passages on standardized tests and in difficult texts that contain comparative language.

We accidently shortchange them by constricting the types of writing we teach and how that writing can be applied to various contexts. Learning to create a poem actually helps a student with essay writing.

The following quotation from poet Mark Doty may be used to initiate a discussion about metaphors; his "definition" may also be applied to teaching the essay or any genre of writing:

> Our metaphors go on ahead of us; they know before we do. And thank goodness for that, for if I were dependent on other ways of coming to knowledge, I think I'd be a very slow study. . . . I need something to serve as a container

> for emotion and idea, a vessel that can hold what's too slippery or charged or difficult to touch. . . . Sometimes it seems to me as if metaphor were the advance guard of the mind; something in us reaches out, into the landscape in front of us, looking for the right vessel, the right vehicle, for whatever will serve.[9]

Giving students time to practice creating their own metaphors will help them identify metaphors in other texts as well as decipher layers of meaning. This is not an easy skill to acquire, and students who have had extensive experience in writing metaphors will become better test takers as well because they are able to read and comprehend figurative language with more skill than before they created metaphors themselves.

Many of the writing experiences in my classrooms are formative in nature, with students' efforts assessed rather than their final products. However, when the time comes for summative assessments and more formal writing assignments, my students know that they have powerful tools—including metaphoric language—to bring to their written arguments.

5

Applications with Prose Poems or Poetic Prose

The prose poem is a natural fit for students exploring discourse through the use of metaphor. The metaphoric language allows them to explore the themes and topics on multiple levels simultaneously.

Assignment: Write a prose poem or poetic prose in which you use at least three metaphors to make an argument about the work of literature you are reading.

Objectives: Comprehend, generate, and apply metaphors to a poetic prose or a prose poem as a tool of analysis and expression

Anna's* poem explores the symbolism of the Fisher King in T. S. Eliot's poem *The Waste Land*. She also experimented with parody and anaphora, using many of Eliot's motifs and playing with his wording (just as Eliot himself did with other writers). In addition, Anna recognizes the relevance of the poem to the world today, to our contemporary politics, our wars, and our fears.

Unreal City
The Unreal City
It lies beyond the spectrum
Of our physicality.
Waiting.
For the Fisher King
Is to lead us to
The Unreal City.
We cannot imagine the horrors there.
Our minds would crumble to dust,

But still we seek the enlightenment.
"Each man fixed his eyes before his feet" (65)
"Under the brown fog" (208)
"Ringed by the flat horizon only" (370)
The Unreal City
Hides. Within the soul of every man
And woman
We go there when we die,
To face our fears
And face our fate.
To show us our
Path. To guide,
Like the Fisher King
The Fisher King displays
What is to come,
Like the Tarot.
The Unreal Cities tell us
How not to be.
So we can live our lives better.
Three Unreal Cities,
Each worse than the last
Foretell the horrors of man.
They show up
In groups of three
I don't know why.
Perhaps to represent
"The third that walks always beside you?" (359)
Maybe not.
The first Unreal City
In section one:
The Burial of the Dead
The monotony of life
Within the machine
Of capitalism.
Trudging off,
Day after day,
Accomplishing nothing.
Also like the spirits
Paying their dues
To cross the Styx.
Is that what it has come to?
We no longer need a ferryman
To carry our souls to salvation?
Have they made a machine for that?
Is there an app for that?
The shame I feel for society.
And the brown fog

Belched from the factories
Chokes the winter dawn.
And we trudge along
With our eyes to the ground,
The way they taught us to.
"I pity the fool"
Who suffers such
And does not say a word.
He will end up
Buried in the garden.
Left only for the dog to dig up.
The second Unreal City
Located conveniently
In The Fire Sermon.
A level of Hell
Reserved solely for
Staunch [Politicians.]
A man
Asking another man
To spend a weekend with him.
Men like men.
Eliot and Verdenal.
Scandalous?
They talk in vulgar slang
And show their obvious secrets.
Comradeship.
Shame or
Secrecy?
Which is the hotter hell?
Homosexuality?
"Nuff said."
Wrong-o, Jack.
Depending on your views
It could go either way.
Just like Eliot.
This is more personal
Than the rest.
Just to be chaotic.
The third Unreal City
What the Thunder Said.
Perhaps the scariest of all.
But not at all.
Reality is sometimes worse
Than fantasy.
When the bats mock you
Because you are sterile
Like a prostitute.

Or the Fisher King.
Both have their ups and
Downs.
Upside down towers
Like that game we used to play
When we were kids.
Upside down towers,
To show that what we think is good
Is just pure evil.
Like an upside down cross
Is a symbol of
The Anti-Christ.
In the name of the Father,
The Son,
And the Holy Ghost.
Ménage a trois.
Yet again.
Eliot was a fun-loving man.
The bats "crawled head downward" (381)
Like Regan in
The Exorcist.
Demonic imagery.
The loss of religion.
World War One.
Upside down towers or
Destroyed cities
Perhaps not so much fantasy.
The spacing of the Cities
Every other section.
My OCD is dancing in the street.
Patterns.
Repetition.
Threes everywhere.
Maybe not so much a general
Three levels of Hell.
But a personal one, for Eliot.
Perhaps the Wasteland
Is his life.
Poor fellow.
His family was middle class.
He had a maybe-perhaps-kinda-not really lover.
He watched Europe implode.
Perhaps the Wasteland
Is (in) his mind.
Poor fellow.
The Wasteland is conveniently
An allegory of his life.

Poor fellow.
He probably felt that his
Life was not worth much.
Poor fellow.
His discontent prompted him
To write in a fashion
Most suiting of his mood.
But it provides
An adequate commentary.
Frankly quite coincidental
To the commentary
Given about the society
Of today.
Maybe Eliot is trying to tell us
That it is moot to try.
I hope not.
Maybe the Fisher King is not
Leading us through
The land of the dead.
Maybe the Fisher King is
Showing the consequences
Of our actions.
It is upsetting
That Fisher King/Jesus/Bran
Is frowning upon me.
S/he crosses time and space
And s/he continues to frown upon
Humanity.
The sad final realization
The Unreal Cities aren't that far off
From the real cities.

Assignment: For this journal entry, you will write a musing, a poem, or a short essay-style prose piece (or another vehicle of your choosing) in which you use metaphors and consider how metaphors work. Your topic: metaphors.

Although this is a "free-write" entry in which the only boundaries are to create or use a metaphor, the students tackle the topic in various ways, exploring the abstraction both in reading and writing. The resulting discussions following this quick exercise lead into discussions with greater depth as a result of the critical thinking students are engaged in through the creative practice of uncovering, discovering, and creating metaphors.

Assignment for a College Freshman Composition Class: Write a 500-word composition in which you explore narrative writing and create at least one metaphor.

Jumping to a higher level of education but not necessarily of student ability, I found great success with metaphor and poetic techniques instruction in my college English 099 composition class. I recall that Tim* walked in the first day of the semester and pronounced his emphatic statement: "I'm not a writer. I'm just trying to get through this." Although an intelligent young man, Tim had not made academics a priority while he was in high school. As a result, his writing skills were deficient, but he caught on quickly when we started working with metaphors.

A couple of weeks into the semester, we were in the middle of a peer-editing activity when I overheard Tim say to another student, "Just add a few metaphors. She'll love those." Of course, the addition of the figurative language also improved the student's writing. Near the end of the semester, Tim handed in his narrative essay with the words, "I can't wait to see what you have to say. This is one of the best things I've ever written." He had written a composition about remodeling an antique truck that served as a symbol for repairing his relationship with his father. The fact that the composition worked so well on two levels brought him a great sense of accomplishment, something, in fact, that he thought he was not capable of doing before taking the writing course.

His composition began with a metaphor that served as a thematic conceit. In many respects, it was the creation of the metaphor that allowed him to move beyond the literal, pushing his writing into complexity and a higher level of expressive thought. He began the semester barely able to meet the minimum requirements for entry into college, and he left the course writing at a solid B level. Although part of his huge leap was due to emotional maturity, he made up the rest with the new skills in creative techniques that he had acquired during the semester.

> **Assignment:** Explore and analyze T. S. Eliot's themes, motifs, and dominant symbols found in *The Waste Land* through a vehicle and format of your choosing. Address the essential questions from our literature exploration in some manner in your writing about Eliot's poem. Your product should be at least two to three pages in length. While you are not required to use a creative format, such as a poem, musing, prose poem, or script, you are encouraged to bring the creative techniques that you have mastered into your writing about Eliot's poem.
>
> **Objectives:** Exploration of Eliot's dominant themes, motifs, and symbols, use of creative technique(s) to express your ideas about Eliot's seminal poem

For an assignment in AP English Literature and Composition, I provided the following parameters for the student writing: explore theme, motif, and dominant symbols in T. S. Eliot's *The Waste Land*. Students were not only allowed but encouraged to use creative approaches in their written product.

Sam* did not consider himself a poet nor had he written poetry on his own. However, he was excited by his writing and the way it brought other students into discussions about not only Eliot's themes but why Sam chose to highlight particular motifs and themes in his poem. While few of my students write with such sophistication, all of them are capable of much deeper thinking and more affecting written product than they were before entering into these exercises in creative techniques, creative approaches, and creative choice.

Sam's* prose poem critically explores symbols, themes, and motifs in T. S. Eliot's *The Waste Land*.

A Guide to the Fisher King: Hope in the Waste Land
Restoration, renewal, rebirth
core conceptual ideas given by
T. S. Eliot in *The Waste Land*
Chaos and complexity, one entity, which engulfs the world in
a sea of abyss, allowing no return
Structuring his poem in a parallel
framework, giving the effect of chaos through
deep waves of motifs, symbols, allusions, and "voices"
Motifs based on antithesis, along with multiple
interruptive voices, the state of humanity based on a chaotic
reality, forming a fragmentation of thought in an in-cohesive society
and metanarrative. The most significant symbol is that of
the Fisher King because of the long history of this archetypal symbol
Symbolism behind this icon is arguably the most complex
in literature
The Fisher King at times can be difficult to follow, yet ironically Fisher
King represents the guide through the waste land. The pilgrimage
encompasses all of light and darkness in a hesitant time period where
the world seems unbalanced and disproportionate
It is clearly apparent that the Fisher King leads us
on a spiritual quest for healing and following our descent into a land
of personal, cultural, and global decay and destruction
For every blooming flower, there is a decaying weed embodying
truth behind Eliot's extensive use of antithesis:
"That corpse you planted last year in your garden, has it
begun to sprout?" (71–72) All symbols have multiple meanings
contributing to the depth and complexity in the waste land.
Generally "planting" a corpse, or dead body is not expected to grow
or bloom; however, Eliot contradicts the general perception
based on imagery by employing the objective correlative
This element of inevitability adds to the principle of complexity
in more than one way
Deciphering *The Waste Land* can
metaphorically be equivalent to a blind man trying to escape a

labyrinth—a task that appears nearly impossible, and as a direct result,
the background of our guide, the Fisher King, must be analyzed and
understood. Originally Celtic, Christian, Pagan, and Chimerical
in origin related to fertility rituals and salvation quests
Symbol that overlaps between Christian and Pagan traditions,
much like the common air we breathe
Ichthys is the most commonly used word in the New Testament for
fish, and that is in many forms the symbol or the Greek for Fisher King
who can take the form of male or female based on the presented situation
This guide is on an eternal quest leading to spiritual enlightenment
that may never be fully obtained. Much like the fires of war that
never seem to be extinguished: the wants and needs of
mankind in a chaotic and unstable world
Bloodshed only brings about more bloodshed
Most unique about this legendary symbol:
Fisher King is always portrayed with a paradoxical
infirmity that is wounded with God-like powers: a healer
of others combined with restorative powers in a reality
known as the waste land
This Fisher King can move
between realms, between life and death, entering a whirlpool
of suffering that may never cease to end

"Datta. Dayadhvam. Damyata." (432)
Give. Sympathize. Control
Once sterile, thunder speaks for God
Fisher King offers spiritual connection:
Earth and the Heavens
A promise for new beginnings
Crumbles all civilization
"Falling Towers,
Jerusalem Athens Alexandria,
Vienna London
Unreal" (372–75)
Once great focal points of culture
Now upside down towers facing hell
"London Bridge is falling down falling down falling down" (426)
Truly splendid destruction erupts
With time comes extermination
Regardless of realization
The rehabilitation of a system of beliefs
Witnesses the Fisher King
A Global vision of the world as
Waste Land awaiting for the arrival of the Grail
A true Cure within reach
"Shantih shantih shantih" (433)
A peace which passeth understanding

Hope present in eternal darkness
Hope existing in Blindness
Hopeful Waste Land
Both violent and radical
Renews the understanding of civilization
Revitalizing mankind
Fisher King presents a rebirth of thought
A restoration of a system of beliefs
Through a principle of complexity
Along with motifs and symbols
Articulate an unorthodox structure Guiding us through the Waste Land
Sehat. Naveekaran. Punarjanam
Restoration. Renewal. Rebirth

Clearly, Sam not only created a prose poem but also an analytical one that explores, imitates without mocking, and considers Eliot's style and techniques as well as the difficult symbolism of the Fisher King. The prose poem as well as the poetry form, in a way, allows students to be able to discuss very difficult subject matter before they can articulate it as well in prose.

6

Discourse Applications with Poetry

Prior to experimenting with nontraditional forms of writing, my students seldom, if ever, referenced the Fisher King in writing about T. S. Eliot's poem. The complexity of the symbol—with its varied origins from diverse cultures—left them frustrated and silent, but the ability to use poetry to suggest rather than overtly state brought this important symbol to the discussion table again. The poetry allowed them entrance to an expression of higher levels of thought, critical thinking, and deeper reading of the text.

> **Assignment:** Through writing, explore the thematic concepts found in one or more of the Confessional poems we read during this unit. If you choose a nontraditional vehicle for your ideas, make sure that you address at least three of the Confessional poetry movement's characteristics. Bring the work of at least two Confessional poets into your written piece. Incorporate at least two poetic techniques in your writing.
>
> **Objectives:** Demonstration of an understanding of at least three characteristics of the Confessional Poetry movement, exploration of themes in two poems, comprehension and incorporation of poetic techniques

The following original student poem explores thematic concepts found in the American literary movement of Confessional poetry. This young man explores and analyzes the relationship between the Confessional poets' lives and their works through his poem. The poem synthesizes the movement's characteristics, several elements from several Confessional poets' biographies, and the topics of their poems as well as the transgressive nature of these themes. Ethan's* poem is rich with allusions, showing knowledge of the poems' lines and the ideas expressed in those lines.

Ethan
EElva
Kerpunk! Kerplank!
Hssss . . .
The children are upstairs.
Our neighbor will be arriving soon.
I know you'll understand.
Water boils to the 212th degree.
Her skin starts to burn the bottom. A pungent, burnt smell.
Mrs. Grasses

God does not exist.
Upside down towers fly high in the distance. Give me a brick, so I can fly my kite in a storm.

The tires swerve left, too far. Lost, alone; urges stir the wheel, Erupting in a phoenix of fire.
Ed is ripped into two.

I am figurative. You are literal. Imaginary. Real.
Elva sees faces around her.
The eyes follow; her heart beats. Abolishing the bright lights,
she moves into their shadows.

Up into the ghostly stairs or
creeping through the menacing hallway.

Walking into the bakery, pricked by thorns. A man walks in.
Words exchanged, but she's cloaked with desire.

Waltzing to and fro, she takes a seat.
The rock hard surface; her chest pronounced and projected forward.

The mind is infantile, too easy to convince, Blighted.
Frosted. Presto.
No dolce. Only forte.

Zzzzzippp.
Feet shuffle closer. Pup. Pup. Pup.
Her blouse falls to the ground.

Sinking into my body. Cold, hard, and sharp.
Liquid pours out, sliding down my skin, forming a pool on the floor of the bakery. I think. You breathe.

Remorse. Regret. Renewal.

Simulations.
We create new relationships. Rosebud cannot help us.

We lie, hate, and feel pain. I've stolen the Jack.
You're trying to shoot the Moon. We'll fail.

Half a decade passes. Laughter. Mockery.
I didn't think of us. Perception.
I'm the Master. You're the slave.

I've done nothing. Been nothing.

When Ostrander swings. I'll fall.

I've been too fortunate.
Ed will arise out of the ashes.

When we encourage our students to create work that deals with the implicit rather than the explicit, they begin to read differently, more deeply. Although the introduction of creative techniques and various creative approaches improves students' writing, this methodology also works—as previously stated—to improve their reading comprehension and critical thinking. Much of what takes place in our classrooms prepares students for comprehension at the literal level, but most texts in high school and beyond offer nonliteral meanings. Students have much less difficulty reading and understanding complex poetry after they have worked on their own poetic creations. They are, quite simply, no longer intimidated by figurative language, symbolism, and allusions. After all, they have been using them in their own writing!

Assignment: Write a short response to *Hamlet* in which you explore characterization. You may choose a nontraditional format for your character exploration/analysis. The length should be approximately one to two typed pages.

Objective: Comprehension of characterization, divergent thinking, self-direction in the creation of a writing project vehicle

Jillian Mitchell's poem was written in response to a character study assignment during our unit on Shakespeare's *Hamlet*. Here, the assignment allowed for creative choice in the writing format. The rubrics were focused on an exploration of characterization in the play. I have found that students love choosing their vehicles as much as their words. In fact, they may love their words more because they have been able to choose the vessel.

Ophelia's Revenge
Words cannot describe all the love there's been
Together, we move into the light, in out of darkness
When you're gone, the light leaves as it is swallowed by darkness
Shadows of hate and madness, deception and lies
The screams of trickery and whispers of promise
Truth of the matter is that love is a falsehood
You were my life and now you are gone
So what is the point of living?
I would have married you
But you were obsessed with your father's death
So much that it tore me away from your thoughts
Did you think, or were you so overtaken by revenge,
That you forgot what we had
Could you not see, that last time we talked, the flicker
Of past love and future loss
Then, now, my love, is the end of us both
You have already left, and I am here, always waiting for you
But you will never come back, so infatuated with another: Revenge
So I go to my death, knowing this world will no longer hold me
I will be free
Goodbye, my Hamlet, and remember
I loved you always or never at all

Jillian clearly takes a position as to the cause and nature of Ophelia's death. It was no accident but a suicide, according to this student of *Hamlet*.

Allan's* poem was written in response to a question about examining heritage, a topic inspired by the Rosamond Gifford lecture series that season. Here is an example of writing in response to nonfiction. We also read the text of the lecture in class.

How, Exactly, Do You Pronounce a Letter in English?
A bitter-sweet sheet of snow covered the ground that particular night
Bitter due to the immense coldness
Sweet due to the knowledge that it would be the last time my
Great grandfather would have to put up with pogroms
With bread-lines
With scarcity of clothing
With starvation

A ticket to America was any Russian-Jew's dream in 1910
A ticket that my great grandfather's own father
Died to give to him
Such an honor to be the Czar's personal tailor
Such an honor to have been shown prejudice
Such an honor to slowly starve to death

"Mother Russia"
Where was your parental comfort during those times?
Why were not your arms extended toward your children?
Where was the food Father Lennon had promised?
Bread, peace, and land
You stole the bread
You disrupted the peace
You burnt the land
Are not Jews people, too?

What did forcing the Jews out of Russia
Accomplish, Mother Russia?
Obviously, it did not halt you
From purging thousands of other people
Obviously, it did not halt you
From taking away individual liberties
Obviously, it did not halt you
From starving your people

My great grandfather saw a boat that day
Perhaps the boat was dilapidated and crowded
But it reflected an aura of freedom
To him, it was a shining boat of hope
A shining boat of promise
A shining boat of beauty
It was his path to a new life
Guffman
Such an odd name
How exactly do you pronounce a letter in English
That is only available in the Russian language?
Hoffman.
Easier to pronounce
And it sounds American
Your new name is Hoffman
A name can be changed
But a culture cannot be,
Mother America
My grandfather's new home
Judaism
Still his culture and religion
A plethora of diversity wherever you look in America
But is not that why it is grand?

Allan's poem reads in many respects like an essay on American diversity.

> Assignment: For this Creative Writing class assignment, you will create a poem that pays homage or tribute to a well-known poet and his or her poem. You may experiment with parody to a degree, but the focus should be tribute, not mocking the poet and poem. Your poem should move beyond mere imitation of the poem to which you are indebted.

The next poem was written by a student in a creative writing class, but he was simultaneously reading works from the AP English class even though he was not enrolled in that class.

T. S. Eliot's lengthy, difficult, and seminal poem *The Waste Land* was originally titled *He Do the Police in Different Voices.*[1] John's* poem in five parts pays homage to Eliot with a multitude of allusions to other poets and philosophers, in addition to playing upon Eliot's unused title. It also incorporates parodic aspects. John's poem was created in a creative writing class although it might easily have been created in my AP English literature class.

John
He Do the Police in Different Voices

"It is the business of the very few to be independent; it is a privilege of the strong. And whoever attempts it, even with the best right, but without being OBLIGED to do so, proves that he is probably not only strong, but also daring beyond measure. He enters into a labyrinth, he multiplies a thousand-fold the dangers which life in itself already brings with it; not the least of which is that no one can see how and where he loses his way, becomes isolated, and is torn piecemeal by some minotaur of conscience. Supposing such a one comes to grief, it is so far from the comprehension of men that they neither feel it, nor sympathize with it. And he cannot any longer go back! He cannot even go back again to the sympathy of men!"
—Friedrich Nietzsche, *Beyond Good and Evil*

"The individual has always had to keep from being overwhelmed by the tribe. If you try it, you will be lonely often, and often frightened. But no price is too high to pay for the privilege of owning yourself."
—Rudyard Kipling, sometimes attributed to Nietzsche

I

"To Keep from Being Overwhelmed by the Tribe"
A young man of about thirteen sits alone on a bus; it is me, the author. In this section, the occupant of the seat in front of him asks him a question.
"Hey," he begins. This kid looks a bit fragile.
". . . ," the author responds. This can't be good, he concludes.
"Do you suck _____?" Probably.
"What?" asks the author—not out of having heard him incompletely or to ask for an explanation of an ambiguity present within the clearly un-ambiguous query, but out of the special kind of incredulity that results from, ironically enough, the expected occurrence. It isn't.
"Do you suck _____?" he repeats, but with a bit of extra flair, as it was. Oh, shit. Look at his face.
". . . No."

"Yes, you do," he says matter-of-factly. Nice try.
And our author does not respond. He is heckled for another few minutes. Our author still does not respond. A for effort in category one, mister, so far.
Let us see what happens within a few short years:
"I love you," says the author, this time not to the occupant of the seat in front of him.
And so he has failed, for he has been overwhelmed. "The door swings both ways," you might say.

II

"To Be Lonely"
What does it mean to be lonely?
Our author waits for his response. He sits in his creative writing classroom, rocking back and forth gently, a wad of sickly-spearmint gum pulsing between his jaws.
I was asking you.
I dunno, she says.
The author asks aloud once again, softer this time. He does not wait for a response, but:
I dunno, she says, bristled this time.
Fine. We're going to find out what it's like to be lonely.
What does it mean to be lonely?
Our author waits for his response. He sits in his creative writing classroom, rocking back and forth gently, a wad of sickly-spearmint gum pulsing between his jaws.
I was asking you.
Our author perks up, because the occupant of the seat in front of him is Friedrich Nietzsche. He responds deliberately and with a German accent. He has not yet gone mad, as he has not yet witnessed the horse he saw being beaten to death. This is because he is not real.
To be lonely is to have an unsatisfying conversation with oneself, he says.
Are you really Nietzsche? (The author would have been smart to read the third sentence preceding this one.)

No. I am a product of your mind.

. . . So, I am technically not lonely, then?
You are not, granted; you are not disappointed by your own façade.
This is . . . counterproductive.
Not the word I would have selected, notes Nietzsche.
The author stares at the man.
I suggest you make the most of your situation regardless.
The author's friend Kurt, curiosity freshly piqued, approaches the two and suggests to the author:
You should ask him something silly. Like something you wouldn't expect a philosophical answer for. You should ask him, like, "why is the sky blue?"
Okay, then. Why is the sky blue?
You have doubly failed now, says Nietzsche.
What? The author has the more conventional sort of incredulity upon him this time.

Not only are you not lonely; you have been overwhelmed by the tribe.
I wanted advice.
Which, by definition, is a violation of my philosophy,
the author responds.
I see you are convinced. They are silent.
You're a good logician, I'll grant you.
Nietzsche acts as if he does not notice the comment, and asks:
Would you like to see why the loneliness of unsatisfactory self-satisfaction, henceforward to be referred to as "true loneliness," is so often confused with the common definition?
Do I have any choice?

III

i

"To Be Frightened"
Where am I? Hello? Goddamit.
Where am I? Hello? Goddamnit.
(He said the second louder
[and a few minutes later].)

He is on a bridge. Beyond
his sphere of influence,
idiot brilliance—
lays many a sorry creature.
Some examples include:

The twin eggs of smoking coal
and dusty ice; guardian mother-bird
feeding on the shrimp-worm's
delicious, delicious, delicious nectar.
But is it nutritive? God knows.

The mother-bird is perched
atop the stinging hydrae;
they gnash, sing songs:
"fatherland, O fatherland,
proud as muck and scum are we."

Sideways, as if by renegade
gravity, a sea of blood,
churning, leaping up and
learning to fly, but never,
never landing.

And the mother-bird sees all,
knows some, does none.
And the man on the bridge knows
this, and, relishing his own quietude,
dies—all with determination.
Where the hell did you take me?

Nietzsche sighs. A painting called Con Brio 4, he says. Rudolf Bauer. 1917. But that is unimportant. What is important is the difference between true and false loneliness.
But you killed me, the author says, with the most incredulity of the three noted instances thereof in this work.
You killed yourself, says Nietzsche, who is actually the author. And the author knows this, because he wrote it, and he responds:
Screw you.
And Nietzsche, hearing this, raises a finger as if a good idea had just occurred to him and says the word subtext, and, s(u-)ddenly s(o)bered, s(h!)rugs.
What?
Not important to you, he sneers, causing an undulation of his moustache.
I know it's not, says the author, but not within the context of his conversation with Nietzsche, but literally, as he sits—I sit—in front of my computer keyboard, knowing more than the author about whom I am writing than he himself does.
As I was saying before, says Nietzsche (now), what is the difference between true and false loneliness?
Well, says the author, acquiescing to the game, I felt lonely, I know that. And scared . . . And then I just died.
What did you see?
Snow.
And that was all?
Yes, but . . . but I knew about other things. Everything there, really.
And why didn't you go and see them?
I don't think I could have.
Yes. You are correct. So is this true or false loneliness?
I have no idea.
Remember the definition of true loneliness.
The author thinks, and then responds: it was true loneliness, wasn't it?
Nietzsche nods. But how did you know about the others?
I just knew.
Did you know from the first moment you arrived?
I suppose not, the author concedes.
Then you were told, as it were. Does that not remove the loneliness?
Obviously not.
And why not?
Because . . . because I couldn't respond?
No.
Because it wasn't verbal?
No! He is growing excitedly agitated. Think!
The author's movements become less fluid, and his eyes look as if they were that of a wounded animal. But he comes to a conclusion in time:
Because they weren't myself.
Yes. Exactly.

ii

"To Own Yourself"
And Nietzsche vanished.
What had the author learned? "I don't know," he says—he said. So he stood, approached the window, and looked upon the outside world, and it was not

present. Yet he knew of its nature—the imagery flooded his mind. The hydrae became rustling grasses, and the eggs the sun, scorching hot, smoking the clouds into existence, and the cold moon, visible as it sometimes is in the daytime sky, and the sideways sea of blood the bricks of the building itself, and the shrimp-worms the flowers and insects nestled among the grass's hydrae's million appendages. But where was the mother-bird?
Come here a second, she said.
And he decided: the mother-bird was whoever he wished her to be.

In addition to meeting the lesson objectives, this creative approach has the direct benefit of empowering and deeply engaging students. After these experimental writing exercises, students have stated that they have become more confident writers and ones who are willing to try different structures and consider alternative perspectives in order to improve their products. It is no longer a question of simply meeting the assignment objectives but about exploring their abilities to create, state, analyze, and consider ideas in myriad ways.

Most students do not begin as poets; rather, they enter the classroom uncomfortable with nonliteral language. One of the most exciting moments as a teacher occurs when a student makes that leap and discovers the metaphor as his or her tool, as well as its power.

The following poem was written by Kurt*, who once said that he didn't write poetry and didn't like poetry. After reading his poem, it is clear that his ability to "read" poetry had taken an enormous leap forward from that first week of class.

Kurt
Let the poem
read you
The poem is the writer now
and you are written
Sometimes it whispers in your ear
Other times it screams for attention

The poem is an artist
Its colors splash into a spectrum of light
like that created by a kid jumping into a puddle
The drops of water hit you
The rest just hit the ground
The poem is a dancer
It dances the dance of life

Watching this young man quietly create the poem as he sat in class, seeing him apply the techniques he had learned, I thought about how they shaped not only his writing but also his thinking. Without question, he left the class not just a better writer but a better reader.

FLEXIBILITY IN ASSIGNMENTS AND ASSESSMENTS

The key to helping students improve their writing—for the writing instructor—is flexibility, that ability to react to students' needs and encourage their interests. It also involves how educators grade students' written "products." Not everything needs nor should be considered a summative assessment. Students work on acquiring skills and techniques in many formative assignments that can be designed to incorporate creativity, building to those summative assessments in which the students bring all of their tools and skills to bear. Before introducing writing lessons, the first question educators should ask is, "What do I want my students to learn?" Make that clear to students, provide great models, and then support their efforts to experiment. Not every poem or attempt at poetry will resonate, but your students will learn far more in the process of making their own decisions about how to convey their ideas rather than having the decisions made for them.

SUMMARY NOTES

Student experiments with metaphor and creative structures—including poetry—for their arguments lead to higher levels of engagement in the writing process, divergent thinking, and better understanding of the texts they are reading.

7

Applications with Narrative—Story, Dialogue, and the Mini-Script

In my college composition class, Tim* handed me his narrative essay in which the restoration of a truck metaphorically mirrored the rebuilding of his relationship with his father. Before he turned it in, he smiled and said, "It's the best piece of writing I've ever done." He was right. I should point out that Tim came into the class insisting that he could not write (as do many of my students on the first day). Although the gradual improvement in his writing paralleled instruction in grammar and mechanics, the leap in his work took place only after the introduction of the metaphor in class and his experimentation with the nonliteral. Without question, he began to spend more time on his writing due to his increased confidence and mastery of techniques. The idea, however, of telling a story in which an argument was embedded excited the students, Tim most dramatically.

During our genre study in AP English Literature and Composition, students were introduced to Virginia Woolf and an excerpt from her seminal work *A Room of One's Own*. The polemic began with Woolf asking her listeners—it was first delivered as a lecture—and readers to consider what would have happened to a woman at the turn of the seventeenth century with the talent of Shakespeare—in fact, Shakespeare's imaginary sister, Judith. At first, the students had difficulty with the fact that a narrative could be embedded in an essay form in order to further or strengthen an argument. Woolf's writing became a revelation for them. Simply reading this excerpt and discussing the ideas generated much experimentation on the part of my students, who were anxious to try using narratives in their essays. I have also used a shorter form of this excerpt in my college composition classroom.

It is important to note here that not every student-initiated writing experiment is successful, any more than every traditional essay by our students is outstanding, but the potential for success and student involvement is much greater when the students take the impetus, feel a sense of ownership of the assignment, have more at stake through their decision making, and are more invested in the outcomes. There has been a great deal of pedagogy written about compliant versus engaged learners, and every teacher wants his or her students to be engaged learners even when compliance is sometimes easier for all of us. With the creative approaches to writing assignments, the results occasionally show only a tangential connection to the assigned task. It is up to us to make sure that students understand the learning goal of a particular assignment and that the goal is clearly articulated. At that point, it is imperative that we give up some control over the assignment and allow our students to make choices. Although not every choice will result in excellence, our students will learn despite or perhaps even through their missteps.

The following composition was written in response to an assignment asking students to consider and analyze the inspiration(s) for the poetry of W. B. Yeats. I expected that they would arrive at some response that involved the concept of beauty and Yeats's dedication to Maud Gonne, the recipient of Yeats's unrequited love.

Jonathan*

Beauty: it has been said to drive a man insane. I can see how it does. Even now, I find myself slipping into agony. Beauty destroyed the great city of Troy and caused men to spiral into insanity. It's no wonder why I find myself falling victim to the power of it. It has been over a year since the rejection, and when I look in the mirror I do not see a man anymore. The creature is unshaven, has dark circles under his eyes, and his eyes are bloodshot. Looking at his physique, one sees that he is malnourished and exhausted. The room around him is similar to that of a rundown shack. The roof leaks and dust is on almost every surface except the mirror. Is that really me? I close my eyes and reopen them with optimism that it was all a hallucination. I stare into the mirror once more.

To my delight, it seemed I was hallucinating. Instead of what used to resemble a corpse, I see a living being. He's clean, well-fed, surprisingly enough; he has a smile on his face. Glancing around him, he sees a woman. She goes up to him, and she is beautiful. Her appearance is perfect in every way imaginable to him. What about her mentality? Does it matter? Her beauty is great enough to obliterate cities without ever lifting one of her fingers. I wonder what my world would be like if I was not with her. I enter a dark recess of my mind for a moment, which I wish to never revisit.

The man in the mirror is exuberant and the envy of all other men. If only he could teach the ignorant men who want this beauty how to obtain her. Then they wouldn't be ignorant, would they? This woman with the man seems to cause others to descend into madness and violence. What is this woman's name, you ask? Some call her Helen, while others call her Maud, or even Ireland. What do you call her? Her name, to me, is irrelevant. She is a mystical and can cause men who do not have her to wage wars. I am thankful that she is by my side. I question what life would be like if she was not mine.

I see a bright flash, and I am back where I was. I am in my apartment, staring at the mirror in the decrepit room. There is no beauty beside me. It was all a daydream. The mind is a powerful tool; it can help us cope, or it can assist with insanity. I begin to question myself. Am I one of the ignorant men who fight others for beauty? Will I ever obtain the woman who possesses such beauty that can annihilate civilizations? And will I become just another person ravaged by beauty? There are so many questions, and I have no answers. I am the Ulster to this Usna who I am infatuated with.

It occurs to me that I have nothing to offer this woman and that I am destined to live my days alone in agony. I cease staring into the mirror and break it. The mirror gives me false hope of a world that does not exist. Bliss can cause a man as much pain as agony. With no alternative, I decide to live the rest of my life in despair with the hope that one day I may be able to attain the beauty.

In reworking my writing assignments to allow for a student's creative choices, I realized that I had to leave certain aspects of the task more open-ended while being very specific about the particular learning goals. What follows is one such writing assignment and the student's response.

The Context Presented to Students: According to Ralph Waldo Emerson, "language is the archive of history." Emerson's theme is echoed by Henry Hitchings in his new work *The Secret Life of Words*, in which he states, "Additions to a language may signal a new political movement, a recent discovery, or a sweeping revision of attitudes. Spotting innovations in language affords us an impression of the changing practical, intellectual, social, and aesthetic needs of society."[1] After studying Shakespeare's wordplay and inventiveness with language in *Hamlet*, you are encouraged to see language as a living representation of communication and relate a word's etymology or history.

The Task: Using *The Oxford English Dictionary* as your guide and source, write an approximately two-page etymology on a single word appearing in *Hamlet*. Before framing your writing, remember to consider Virginia Woolf's narrative of Judith Shakespeare within her feminist treatise. Your "essay" may be as inventive as you like as long as your response is aligned with accurate information about the word's history from the dictionary. Your word essay should allude to or directly state definitions of the word and its first known use.

Excerpt from the Work of Lydia*
The Great Adventures of Visage
It all started about 1300 in Europe; it was there where Visage was born, a delicate, beautiful baby girl. Upon her birth, an evil spirit came to curse this poor babe. Her life would only last as long as Visage was known, or the darkness from inside old musty books forever left on a bookshelf would consume her. The evil spirit Dictionaria granted her a few years to become known and grow before this curse would take effect. Terrified, the girl's parents, Culture and Vernacular, told her the meaning of her name from that day forth until she was old enough to understand its meaning and until she was ready to go out into the world on her own. "Visage," they would say to her, "your name means the face, the face with reference to the front part of the head of a person; go and one day let people make use of your good and feminine name, for one day it will save your life." Visage was known by her family and friends and continued to live on.

Julia's* narrative "essay" extends the literature, asking the reader to consider what became of Caddy Compson in William Faulkner's *The Sound and the Fury*. In asking my students to look for the voice of the only Compson child to be denied a narrative section, I was asking students to read analytically, think about narrative in ways they had not previously considered, and imagine how the conversation might continue.

Julia
White Flame Ladies
She was so good last night; I cannot even describe the feeling. She is like a fine wine, man; she gets better with age, and I am a thirsty boy. I know she has all those fine little things that she runs around like a mother hen, but I just cannot get enough of that sweet body. I love her southern twang, too; it is like listening to a fine country radio station. I do not quite know where she is from, but I wish I knew how she managed to get herself to Chicago. Such a beautiful woman for a beautiful city; her eyes sparkle like the street lamps. Sometimes I ask her about her life before now, and she just gets this cloudy look in her eyes and drifts off for seconds of time. One time, I asked about her family, and she cried. I asked if she wanted to talk about it, so she wiped her eyes, took in a deep breath, and began to unravel a Southern tale about "family."

I do not want to keep you too long, Manfred. Honestly, I wish I could charge you for this precious time, but seeing as I do not get as many suitors as I have been in the past few years, and seeing as we are such good friends, I can allow this. I must originally lay out to you my family history. Firstly, I will describe to you my two parents. Jason Compson, a man of a wealthy Southern family, married my mother, who was born a lowly Bascomb. I know she hoped that marrying my father would change her social standing in that town, but as time went on, it became the complete opposite. She managed to drag him down with her, always feigning sickness in order to gain everyone's attention. And the fact that he was an alcoholic didn't make it any easier for any of us. Maybe if she had stepped up as a mother, she would have felt more fulfilled in her personal life. Every day in and out she would call for Dilsey, and that woman became her lifeline to our family. Then there's my blessed brother Quentin, who I miss as dearly as my father. He took his own life in 1910 for whatever reason he felt necessary. He was usually right about things because he understood how the world worked and how the Compsons fit into the scheme of all things. He cared so dearly for me. He could feel when I hurt and would always try to heal my sorrows, to fulfill his own code. He even admitted to incest with me in order to give my soon-to-be daughter Quentin a father. I feel partially responsible for his death, maybe had I been there for him, like a shadow keeping him safe, he would still be here with us.

Dear please wipe your eyes I can't bear to see you cry.

It's fine really; I just miss him so. Then Jason, who I wish would have taken his life over Quentin. Even though I have very few burdens, he is one that I doubt I will ever lose. He is determined to make every part of my life miserable now because I "ruined his future" by not marrying Herbert. If he couldn't build a future for himself, I don't see how I was expected to do it for him, a mere girl of seventeen. I can't be expected to save everyone, even though I acted like his or her mother, I just simply wasn't. Finally Benjy, my youngest brother who had the biggest heart of all, but unfortunately could never communicate how loving he truly was. Though he was of mental instability, he knew and felt things that not everyone around us could feel. He had trinkets that would calm him, things that had once been mine that he latched onto for comfort, but when he got upset he would just moan and cry until I came around for him. I can just hope he fares all right without me there because it hurts my heart just to think of him without a motherly figure to keep him happy. Like I said, Dilsey is there, though, and all of her kin probably have a sharp eye on Benjy at all time because it's what they've lived with forever, and there is no point now for them to change. Except for the surely tortured Benjy, I wish I could cut all communication with my family, but my beloved daughter, who I have not yet had the chance to meet face to face, is in the custody of her uncle. I named her Quentin after her late uncle. I wish I could receive a letter from her, just once so she could tell me about the young woman she has become today. I fear I will never get to know the woman that she has become, and that is where my sadness derives from. Jason has been so spiteful, and he's used Quentin as a weapon against me in order to keep feeding him my money while he just takes it. I know he takes it, but I hope he gives at least some of it to her. I know this is a lot to keep up with at once, but since you are so willing to stay here with me, I must assume that you do not mind sitting here longer.

No Candace, I can wait all evening; I really don't mind. I love listening to you talk; your voice is like church bells.

Don't speak about church bells, Manfred; I can't bear the talk of marriage. After being expelled from my family, I worked my way up north, trying to find my place in society the best I could with the skill set I had. Being only good at two things, which were having sex and being a mother, I had very limited means of keeping myself monetarily sound while still sending money to my daughter in Mississippi. After coming to Chicago and seeing the opportunity it presented me, I was able to combine my two skills and run my own home for women. They are all well taken care of, as you can see, and they are just using their skills as I had used mine. My family never really recognized my skills, and I mean it's not necessarily something you're willing to share with your neighbors. I can't complain about it really, but I feel like my maternal instincts should have been recognized. I tried and tried to take over the role that my mother left to Dilsey, the lead help of my family, but I only failed in her eyes. I wish I would have spoken up more now. I may have still been with my family, may have been able to live a "normal" life. I would have loved to have settled down with a man like Herbert, but I have such a roaming heart, I can't manage to remain monogamous.

I think the way you live your life is beautiful Candace.

No, Manfred, it is terrible; I hate how I live, but it's the only way I know how.

Then find a man to start a family with, I mean you and I could always—

No, Manfred, I'm stuck in this lifestyle, you don't understand. I feel like I had so much love to give when I had the opportunity, and now that everyone has thrown me away, I don't want to love anyone else. This physical relationship I continue with you is just because I've had you for so long, and there is no point in having you go with the younger girls. Maybe, had someone listened to me when I was younger, I wouldn't be as hardened as I am now. I don't feel as if nature intended me to live the life I live right now, I blame lack of nurturing for my unconventional lifestyle. I can't change society, but had my parents treated me with more love and respect, I think I would not have relied so heavily on the "love" of others. I yearned for years for that kind of attention parents are to give to their children, and I'm glad that I found it, whether it be socially acceptable or not. I love making love, and it makes me feel like I am important even for that given amount of time.

Do you ever miss them?

Of course I miss them, Manfred. I can't think of a day that goes by without thinking about Benjy's sweet moaning. And Quentin, he always tried to protect me; he thought I was fragile even though I wasn't. Jason, I don't miss. If Jason died today, I would be completely all right with it. I miss Dilsey and her motherly quality. She was the best mother I could have had, and I appreciate her. I feel like she never hears that, and if I could get a letter to her, I would tell her how much she's meant to me over the years.

She took in a deep sigh; the clock began to chime for one a.m.

Manfred, it's one a.m.; I must implore that you leave, so I can get some kind of business tallying done to see if I've made a profit yet tonight or not. I hope your wife is well, and you know my door is always open for you.

Thank you, Miss Candace. I hope getting some of this off of your chest made you feel better. I really enjoyed tonight. As normal, I should be back next Saturday night. Goodnight.

He closed the door, and Caddy got up and opened her closet. She knew she would have to check on the girls in a moment because they should be getting paid shortly. She moved all of her hatboxes to the side and reached for a worn, white slipper that had taken a yellow color with age. She sat down, her back against the bed. With the slipper in her arms, almost being cradled like a baby, she rocked back in forth, singing and crying, reliving walking back through the gate, up the walk between the pear tree and the house, and up into the house. She saw in her mind's eye Benjy sitting in the kitchen, Dilsey sitting there feeding him a hot meal. She felt the door swing as she walked into the dining room, seeing the legacy of what had been her family left behind around that oak table, a warm meal in the center, and the faces blankly staring at Caddy; almost like a walking eulogy.

Kara LaBarge incorporated a diary within a more traditional essay form. Her creative experiment was particularly effective because she had an interest in psychology as well as the literature. This response centers on the task assignment of finding Caddy Compson's voice in William Faulkner's novel *The Sound and the Fury*. Unlike her brothers, who each narrate a section of the novel, Caddy does not have her own chapter, but she is the character whom all of the other characters revolve around. Kara's creative rhetoric explores that silent voice, extending the literature as well as deeply reflecting on Faulkner's novel.

Kara
The Character Diary

May 2, 1898

We played in the branch today. I took off my dress to feel the water. It was cool but felt good even if it made my bodice and drawers stick. Quentin splashed a lot and I splashed back. Versh was gonna tell on us, but I told him "I'll run away" (19) if he tell. Then Maury cried and I had to stop him so I told him "I'm not going to run away" (19). I hate when Maury gets sad. Jason was all by himself. We had to get home so I says "I'm not going slow" (20) to Quentin. When we saw Father Jason tattled. We ate in the kitchen but I knew it wasn't right. Then Frony says "Your grandmammy dead as any nigger can get, I reckon" (33). I wanted to see it so I climbed a tree to see the people in the house. I felt the sadness. It made me sad too.

In William Faulkner's *The Sound and the Fury*, Benjy's first-person narrative provides the least biased opinion of Caddy. For example, when watching Caddy play in the branch, Benjy says, "Some of it splashed on Versh and me and Versh picked me up and put me on the bank" (18). Benjy's passive language indicates his mental disorder, but it is stylistically important as well. English is an egocentric language because the use of the word "I" indicates an individual carrying out an action, yet in other languages, individuals are acted upon. Thus, Benjy's passive narrative stresses his lack of egocentrism and bias.

From Benjy's central consciousness, Caddy is perceived as a loving, mother-like figure. Benjy's dependence on Caddy is evident throughout the novel. Benjy's travels with Luster remind him of Caddy; certain senses such as touch, sight, and sound evoke memories. For example, Benjy's direct discourse reminisces his time spent with Caddy crawling through the garden fence. Luster complains, "'Cant you never crawl through here without snagging on that nail.' Caddy uncaught me and we crawled through" (4). Through Benjy's fixed internal point of view, Caddy is continually the focal character.

The bond between Benjy and Caddy is exemplified when Caddy is playing in the branch. Caddy's threat to run away—a foreshadowing of her future—troubles Benjy tremendously. He narrates, "Caddy was all wet and muddy behind, and I started to cry and she came and squatted in the water" (19). Later on, when Caddy climbs the tree to peek into the main house, Benjy notes her muddy drawers again, "We watched the muddy bottom of her drawers" (39). Caddy's muddy drawers are one of several symbolic references to her fall from grace.

Benjy's section utilizes anaphora to emphasize the motif of Caddy's loss of innocence. For instance, after Caddy kneels next to Benjy and hugs him, he notes, "She smelled like trees" (9). Later at the branch, Caddy reassures Benjy she will not run away and he states, "Caddy smelled like trees in the rain" (19). Benjy also recognizes Caddy's promiscuity by the presence of perfume; "She took up the bottle and took the stopper out and held it to my nose. 'Sweet. Smell. Good.' I went away and I didn't hush, and she held the bottle in her hand, looking at me. 'Oh.' she said. She put the bottle down and came and put her arms around me" (42). Both Caddy's muddy drawers and perfume are symbolic representations of the ill consequences of her sexual encounters.

November 20, 1909

Mrs. Candace Ames. Mrs. Candace Dalton Ames. Dalton Ames. Dalton Ames. Dalton Ames. His name rolls off my tongue. Ames. I like him, and he's good company. I wish everyone else thought so. Today was a nice day, though. Dalton came for me in the morning and we took a buggy into town. Then he bought me pretty violets from the corner girl. Their scent was intoxicating and the stems were smooth in my hand. We walked around town—his hand in mine—to look at the shop windows. Later we went to swim in the branch. I love the feel of water on my skin. I was only in my undergarments, but I didn't care who saw because the water felt so refreshing. Dalton kept looking at me. I wondered what it would be like to make love. I'm not sure if I love Dalton, but I do enjoy his company. I figured that was enough. Still, I couldn't face Benjy when I got home. He kept looking at me and following me around the house with tears in his eyes. But I'm older now. I'm a woman now.

Faulkner's second section truly demonstrates Caddy's power over her brother Quentin. Quentin's figurative language exemplifies his reverence for Caddy. In his dormitory, he reminisces about his sister's wedding day: "That quick her train caught up over her arm and she ran out of the mirror like a cloud, her veil swirling in long glints her heels brittle and fast clutching her dress onto her shoulder with the other hand, running out of the mirror the smells roses roses the voice that breath o'er Eden. Then she was across the porch I couldn't hear her heels then in the moonlight like a cloud, the floating shadow of the veil running across the grass, into the bellowing" (81).

Symbolism is also evident in Quentin's recollection; roses are representative of Caddy's lust. Honeysuckle is also a repetitive reference in Quentin's section. For example, while walking with the lonely girl from the bakery, Quentin recalls one night spent sitting on the porch: "getting the odor of honeysuckle all mixed She would have told me not to let me sit there on the steps hearing her door twilight slamming hearing Benjy still crying Supper she would have to come down then getting honeysuckle all mixed up in it" (129). Honeysuckle hints at Caddy's shame for her promiscuity. Also, Quentin's section frequently omits punctuation to create a stream of consciousness narration. Soon, Quentin describes Caddy in a manner that hints at a Freudian relationship. Quentin justifies himself, "You know what I was doing? She turned her back I went around in front of her the rain creeping into the mud flatting her bodice through her dress it smelled horrible. I was hugging her that's what I was doing. She turned her back I went around in front of her. I was hugging her I tell you" (137). Through Quentin's central consciousness, guilt concerning his feelings for his sister is evident.

Quentin's repetitive justification of his physical contact with Caddy emphasizes his chivalrous attitude about women. While walking with the Deacon, he mentions, "Father and I protect women from one another from themselves our women" (96). This line demonstrates Quentin's sense of responsibility for Caddy. In his first-person narrative, Quentin struggles with Caddy's disgrace of the family. His perspective is clouded by his psychological assertion of Caddy as a physical manifestation of Southern values. For instance, Quentin remembers lying to his father to protect Caddy: "I dont know too many there was something terrible in me terrible in me Father I have committed Have you ever done that We didn't we didn't do that did we do that" (148). Faulkner uses direct discourse to expose Quentin's thoughts, which are exemplified by lack of punctuation and apostrophes in contractions. Anaphora is used again with this phrasing, emphasizing Quentin's guilt. One of Quentin's most pivotal lines occurs during his direct discourse, "On the instant when we come to realise that tragedy is second-hand" (116). This line foreshadows Quentin's suicide and Caddy's exile, when they are both finally able to escape the constraints of the past.

August 5, 1911

I am distraught. My beautiful daughter is no longer with me and I hope I made the right choice. Sometimes I regret my youthful curiosity, but I will never regret having Quentin. She saved me from myself, and perhaps, she might have been able to save my beloved brother. I think her return to home will give her the life I cannot provide. Oh, how I love her.

Jason's section is nearly as biased as Quentin's section in regard to Caddy, yet with disdain—not obsession. Faulkner uses vulgar language to demonstrate Jason's bitter character. In the opening paragraph, Jason says, "Once a bitch always a bitch, what I say" (180). Jason's distaste for Caddy is based on her disgrace of the family name, as well as his loss of employment opportunity. Jason, in contrast to Quentin, blames Caddy for his misery. This section is much easier to relate to because its language is more concrete, rendering Jason's ideas much more tangible. His section is filled with angst, which from the onset makes his character seem truly despicable. However, this raw anger reflects what makes all of us human: our imperfections.

In the fourth and final section, a neutral omniscient narrator hardly mentions Caddy directly. Instead, Caddy is alluded to by her daughter Quentin's presence. Quentin's departure from the Compson household marks the complete erosion of the Compson name. Initiated by Caddy's promiscuity, the fall of the Compson name is furthered by Quentin's disappearance. In the end, Caddy's voice transcends her youth and persists through Quentin. Quentin is able to finally escape from the Compson household and consequently, from the past and old Southern values.

April 10, 1928

I have found out where my mother is living. I wonder if she will recognize me. After all, I was only a year old when she left. Still, I must look something like her. Uncle Ben always cries when he looks at me; it scares me. But I think he just sees my mother, Caddy.

During our class discussions following writing conferences, one student became intrigued with the idea of writing a medical diagnosis in order to analyze Shakespeare's character Hamlet. The young man later shared his writing with the rest of the class, leading to an extended discussion in which we delved into the psychology of Hamlet. The student who wrote the diagnosis took creative risks and seemed more willing to try new techniques and structures in his writing after his success with this character analysis in an unusual framework. In addition, he actually indirectly encouraged other students to experiment with their rhetoric and enriched our class discussions. Teachers are always looking at ways to encourage students to read one another's words and consider the ways the writing opens the texts for them as well.

Reading Bruce Pirie's *Reshaping High School English,* I was struck with recognition of my students' creative approaches to the essay task:

> Theorists describing the active role readers play in making sense of a text often speak of how we "negotiate" or work through "transactions" with whatever is on the page. We can make that abstraction more concrete by literally asking students to enter into a conversation with some aspect of the text. This can happen in two different ways: an interview with a character or an interview with an author.[2]

Simon's* work features anthropomorphism, metaphor, and symbolism, as well as exploration of transcendentalism and thematic concepts found in the authors' texts. The italicized lines are incorporated quotations from Henry David Thoreau and Annie Dillard, as indicated in the student's footnotes.

Simon

Annie Dillard Dreams of Horses

CLIPITTY, CLOPITTY. CLIPITTY, CLOPITTY.

It is morning as the sound of a horse's hooves echo across the grassy fields near the stables. Inside the stables lie mountains of hay and buckets of water. The gate is wide open as a horse has just escaped.

The horse gallops from the stables across the grassy hill, which is surrounded by a small wooden fence. The horse pounds upon the earth with every step, bounding across the yard. The horse leaps over the wooden fence and continues on its way. The horse runs across a busy road, paining its legs with every step upon the hard cement, finally arriving at its destination.

There sits a sparkling pond, full of life, birds singing in the trees. The scent of wild life permeates the summer air. Among the beautiful view, there are park benches erected at the water front. Beer cans lie crumpled at the base of bushes. Motor-cycle tracks are left throughout the park.

As the horse searches amongst this sight, it suddenly sees two eyes peering out of the woods beyond the pond. With curiosity, the horse trots over to the woods. As the horse gets closer, it soon realizes that another horse lives amongst these woods.

The Horse

(trying not to ward off this unknown horse) "Wait, I do not wish to hurt you."

She shuffles backward, trying desperately not to frighten the unknown horse. His sharp ears perk up, listening to the nearby sounds, before slowly retreating into the woods. Suddenly, he reappears.

The Mystery Horse

"Who are you?"

The Horse

"They call me Annie. And you?"

The Mystery Horse

"I call myself Thoreau."

As the horse moves out of the woods, his appearance is revealed. As the sunlight shines down upon them, his black coat glistens. His muscles are taut and strong underneath this thick coat, but his eyes show the despair of age.

Annie stares at him in disbelief. She has never such a beautiful horse. Her own coat is a muddy brown with white patches splotched across her stomach and legs. She is just like all of the other stable horses, not looking any more unique than the next. Her face and eyes show determination.

Annie

"Where do you come from?"

Thoreau

I went to the woods because I wished to live deliberately, to front only the essential facts of life, and see if I could not learn what it had to teach, and not, when I came to die, discover that I had not lived.[3]

Annie

"I escaped from my stables up beyond that highway." (motioning with her head toward the stables). *I would like to learn, or remember, how to live. I came here not so much to learn how to live, frankly, to forget about it.*[4]

Thoreau

"Out here in the woods, you can learn to forget."

Annie

"Back at the stables, it took me a long time to realize what ideas I should hold on to. My owners gave me plentiful amounts of food; they gave me a nice shelter to sleep in that sheltered me from the cold and rain; they treated me well. But I knew I wasn't happy living that life. After all the comforts they gave me, I stuck with the idea of some day getting out, even though it was comfortable there. And now that I'm here, I'm wishing I could go back."

Thoreau

"Long ago, I lived in a forest of strong oaks and towering pines. I stayed there for many years, galloping through the woods, soaking in the scene around me. *An afternoon sufficed to lay out the land into orchard, woodlot, and pasture, and to decide what fine oaks or pines should be left to stand before the door.*[5] These men came before this precious land and transformed it into a home to keep them warm and give them comfort. They will never be able to repay what they did to the land, but they will continue to perish nature's paradise.

"I once heard through powerful gusts of the wind and the murmurs of the trees at night that *a horse is rich in proportion to the number of things which he can afford to let alone.*[6] (neighing loudly) Drop your saddles, forget the vast amounts of hay, and vanish from the warm shelter. You will live a happier, richer life out in the wild without all of these materials. There is no need for these."

Annie

"I find need for these, though. How will I survive in the wild? Rain, wind, and cold will touch my skin. I will not be able to live out here without the warmth of a stable."

Thoreau

"How can you live your life in a stable? You cannot feel the wind run its soft fingers through your hair. You cannot feel the dew on grass upon your hooves, nor can you feel differences in air as a storm approaches."

Annie

"How will I find food out here? I will die! The idea of living out here captivates my mind, but I would never be able to sustain myself in the wild. I need to stay with my owners to survive."

Thoreau

"*What is a stable, but a seat—better if a country seat.*[7] Your stable provides you with a place to stay, but wouldn't it be better if you stayed within the wild as a huge, vast stable?"

Annie

"Is it possible for us to live in these woods, away from civilization?"

Thoreau

"We have the choice to live any way we want. *Our life is frittered by detail,* so we must *simplify, simplify.*[8] We cannot go through life with hundreds of problems; we should go with one, two, or even none. We do not need stables to keep us warm when we have nature. Possessions are not necessity, so we can get rid of them."

Annie

(twisting her hoof in the dirt in agreement)

Thoreau

"*By closing the eyes and slumbering, and consenting to be deceived by shows, stallions establish and confirm their daily life of routine and habit everywhere, which is built on purely illusory foundations. Colts, who play life, discern its true law and relations more clearly than stallions who fail to live it worthily, but who think that they are wiser by experience, that is, by failure.*[9] Most stallions and mares live life in the stables, giving up their choice to the owners. They live comfortably like you did with food and water, but they did not notice anything. It is amongst the colts and foals, like you, who understand this world. When you are young, you notice everything you see, looking with a curious eye, but then when you get older, the novelty of the experience will wear off. You'll end up forgetting everything."

Annie

"Before, I never thought surviving in the wild would be possible, but now not *even death* can stop me from trying my hardest. My *eyes will burn out and drop* before I give up."[10]

As Annie lifts her head up, her eyes meet Thoreau's black eyes. Their gaze locks like the final puzzle piece. Annie can feel his power and influence. Annie tries to unearth more reasons in his eyes before she realizes the gaze has been broken. Thoreau has disappeared into the woods. First following his hoof prints, her horseshoes sink deeper into the mud, overlapping the trace of his shallow marks.

The following excerpt from Matt's* nontraditional academic essay is structured so that the characters from two texts—the film script from Francis

Ford Coppola's *Apocalypse Now* and Joseph Conrad's *Heart of Darkness*—engage in a conversation with one another in order to critically explore characterization, analyze themes, and offer comment on intertextuality. Coppola stated that he was indebted to Conrad's novella, and the students previously engaged in discussions about imperialism and how texts from different time periods can still mirror ideas and even, in this case, characters; Coppola used the name Conrad for his central, mysterious character.

Matt

"Hello, Walter E. Kurtz. My name is Kurtz, and I am your predecessor; we have much to discuss."

What follows is a clever dialogue between two characters who are at once the same, a sort of schizophrenic view of the nature of identity in these two works of art one, in which Coppola reconfigures and imagines a more contemporary Kurtz in Cambodia during the Vietnam War. The essay begins with a boat slowly making its way down a river as Kurtz waits for Walter E. Kurtz. My AP English former student created a dialogic essay of comparative analysis on characters found in two mediums.

The concepts explored in this writer's essay actually dictated the construct in which the two characters gradually reveal themselves and come to startling conclusions about characterization and themes centered on identity and alienation.

Matt

"Now I think you understand enough," said Kurtz. "There is no need to continue further as you have shared the details with me to prove I can correct . . . It is time for me to go, and it will be your turn to greet the newcomer." Kurtz then slowly evaporated as silence engulfed Colonel Walter E. Kurtz. Though thoroughly shaken by these proceedings, E. Kurtz knew he had a new purpose. Even in death, his previous military training had taught him to always follow his purpose. He knew he was to wait until the next version of Kurtz came along. As he was pondering this notion, he thought he could see a boat slowly trudging toward him and was relieved that he would not have to wait long.

SUMMARY NOTES

Storytelling—one of the most natural forms of creativity—offers an engaging entrance for students attempting to analyze difficult texts.

8

Applications with Parody and Satire

After reading Jonathan Swift's essay *A Modest Proposal*, several students became intrigued with the possibilities inherent in the satire and parody. One of my students chose to create a parody within a mini-script as her structure for her essay about a word's etymology. We discussed the etymology of words in our study of *Hamlet*. She chose the word *court*.

Rose*
LAW AND ORDER: ASE (Another Shakespeare Essay)
Cue Voice over: "In ***William Shakespeare***'s plays, a word often represents two or more separate meanings, yet all definitions are equally important in understanding the text. The words used throughout ***Shakespeare***'s plays are layered deep in puns, and some words were coined by Shakespeare himself. These are their stories."
Cue Music: *Dun Dun Dun*
The setting is outside a court house in New York City. Recess has just been called, and people are pouring outside into the courtyard. Lawyer Kourt is going through her papers with a look of dismay upon her face; it has just been announced that her client is being charged with manslaughter.
Kourt looks over and sees her coworker Henry VI walking toward her.

Henry VI (Trying to start a conversation)
Did you know that a *courtyard* in Ancient Rome was called a *Curia*?
(Kourt rolls her eyes and ignores his random attempt to create a conversation with her. She continues searching through her paperwork as if the solution to the case would appear to her as a picture appears in a child's pop-up book. She finally looks up at Henry VI.)

Kourt

Henry, I am sorry, but I have no time for your random facts. I am trying to get a man off of a possible life sentence.

Henry VI

If only he was as good at *courting* women as he is on the basketball *court*.

(Henry is referring to the case, for Kourt's client is New York Knicks' basketball star Opheil Romeo; Romeo is being accused of killing a prostitute.)

(Kourt turns toward Henry.)

Kourt (Aggravated)

Why don't you stop acting like the *court* fool and actually do something helpful for once? You knew today was a *court* day, and you did nothing to help me prepare. You decided this guy was guilty from the beginning. What, did you place a bet that the Knicks were going to lose their season? Are you trying to keep him out of the game so you can win a few bucks?

(Kourt suddenly stops her arguing. She goes back into the files she is holding and finds the paper she is looking for. Kourt smiles. Henry VI, not realizing the discovery she has made, begins to apologize.)

Henry VI (Apologetic)

Hey . . . *Kourt,* I am really sorry about not taking the case seriously. I am sure you will find a way to prove Opheil's innocence and . . .

Kourt

You remember what you were saying about Ancient Rome earlier? Well, I think we have a situation similar to the assassination of Julius Caesar, and I have just found our Brutus.

End Scene

Henry VI is a play written by Shakespeare in 1599. Shakespeare was the first to coin this particular use of the word *court* in his play *Henry VI.*

David's satiric response to a writing task related to the study of Samuel Beckett's play *Waiting for Godot*. It was also framed as a parody, and he focused on an analysis of Lucky's monologue at the heart of Beckett's tragic-comedy. His response so closely mimics the style, themes, and even the wording of Beckett's existential play that it is helpful to have a copy of the play at hand while reading David's parody/satire. The lack of punctuation is part of the parody and style through which Beckett so challenged his readers and audiences.

David

A title Beckett finds great importance in titles his characters puns playing with language are not literal names Waiting for Godot too straight forward in need of creativity change the longer the better does not work the same with titles

WAIT!
wait for what for Godot of course for who Godot who is Godot someone we need to wait for why do we wait for Godot of course the monologue the reason for speaking existentialist ideas Lucky informs the world of the problems individuality defining everything words words isolated clearer meaning and creation of themselves symbols characters prisms upside down and backwards confusion perplexed inability to see blind dead but there is still hope climbing the mountain side rough hard and frustrating anger but courage venturing deeper into the cave searching for answers not knowing where to go aware believing solutions exist writers discuss and employ morals into characters symbols diction lack of fluid a stream water crashes into rocks diverting more confusion perplexed wonder where what why what again discovering meaning impossible truth never is a full set each apple is bitten but never the whole tree in Absurdia *tennis football running . . . autumn summer winter winter tennis of all kinds hockey of all sorts penicillin . . .* (l. 28–31) random but not quite fate destiny there is always a reason a purpose for existence Samuel Beckett wrote for a reason the seasons and cycles we will ask questions confusion ask more confused again a never ending cycle obtaining knowledge more more wanting the need realization of failure never fully grasping unable all the will strength fails confusion unknown *but not so fast and considering what is more . . .* (l. 11–12) struggling shouting screaming for help reaching absurdity continue to question forcing minds to think writers combine morals characters and symbols into one always almost always no other reason to write maybe for pleasure but there are lessons morals trying to teach scarcity of speech the dialogue more clearly presents defines him Lucky weak inferior inability to speak choice decision to remain silent as the night philosophical metaphorical our people mankind rushing slow down now not thinking unaware missing everything standing back no need to rush cowering in the shadows of superiors ideas thoughts roam birds and bees buzzing singing part of us wants to revolt losing the will to be individual wait shouts wait screams wait struggling revolting standing up the soldier drops his gun refusing to shoot will the rest follow Lucky utters these words with reason what more is there after being mute deciphering the structure language *quaquaquaqua outside time without extension who from the heights . . .* (l. 3–4) words words are not definite relative to the reader pre-existent knowledge creates emotions meaning feelings certain words phrases do not have as much significance as words words alone experiences memememememories help decode but where do we start where to do we end no periods no commas no rules for us to follow Beckett is aware choosing diction structure causing confusion grouping words together to form phrases we think are correct interpretations differ from mind to mind *Given the existence . . . of a personal God . . . with white beard . . . outside time . . . who from the heights of divine . . .* (l. 2–3) logical sense searching for combinations everything can be different *. . . as uttered forth in the public works of Puncher and Wattmann . . . without extension . . . are plunged in torment . . . in fire whose fire flames . . .* (l. 1–8) our mind

sees words in different arrangements based upon emotions memories experiences may be unknown may be unfinished still projecting importance letters letters build words creating language to be able to express ideas more clearly concise and in depth controlling allows for more power Lucky having rarely talked cannot voice his thoughts incoherently describing with ideas colliding not enough practice with language Lucky is does not have control uttering his first thoughts articulation fails his connection is unfinished basic elements materials all parts alone are describable but together Lucky heart stars and horseshoes does not fit the jigsaw pieces together *fire . . . hell to heaven so blue still and calm so calm with a calm* . . . (l. 9–10) simplistic ideas almost there but the thoughts drift from one to another never finishing his mind metonyms a part symbolic of the whole . . . *on the beard . . . the skull the skull the skull* . . . (l. 56–58) the beard of the God as culture describes and skulls symbolizing death without directly describing poison or murder his mind remains simplistic just the same resuming to laughter and humor *Fartov and Belcher . . . Testew and Cunard . . . Possy of Testew and Cunard* . . . (l. 20–22) questioning continue questions to finish at the line realizing the beginning has become the end a cycle again along the way some answers are solved but not all and never will be confusion frustration urge to give up but mind still wonders why Beckett chose one word over another is it possible the monologue is nothing but gibberish are we searching for an answer look to Jacob that actually exists or are the answers intangible thoughts continue running through our heads even after we finish is Beckettkettkett aware does he hold truth within his writing will anyone ever discover his meaning and if they do how will they realize their interpretation is correct Beckett kept a secret of Godot but may not even know the answer himself the only solution to this problem is simply to Wait for Godot.

The following analysis parodies the sexist writer subtly mocked by Virginia Woolf in *A Room of One's Own*; the creative essay simultaneously offers insight into the literature of Henry David Thoreau and Annie Dillard. During class, we had examined great models of the essay and had read Woolf, Thoreau, and Dillard, among others. This young man's creative approach offered opportunity to consider the works and the irony in the tone of each writer, as well as use irony and create an intertextual parody. He was undaunted by the complexity of his task because he was allowed to creatively examine the literature.

Steven*
Letters Regarding the Preposterousness of Weasels and Walden

To Mr. J. Steves,

Upon my flight across the Atlantic, an article within an old, worn flight magazine caught my attention. The article, the name of said text escapes my short-term memory, explored an odd philosophy called Transcendentalism. Essentially, the philosophy (if you wish to call it that) is of early nineteenth century thought and is most commonly characterized by the writers resorting to the instincts found in nature to develop a more purposeful meaning for living. To make sense of the ideals of the philosophy, the article provided two transcendentalist pieces of literature: *Living Like Weasels* by Annie Dillard and *Walden* by David Thoreau. Despite being considered essays (far too long for a man with pressing business matters if you want my opinion) describing basic transcendentalist ideals with different styles, both texts are written for specific audiences in vastly different eras and use different elements of style accordingly.

As previously stated, Dillard and Thoreau both wrote their stories to express ideals of transcendentalism. The two authors explore the instinct and the lifestyle associated with living by bare necessity. Dillard, to illustrate the contrast of human nature and the nature that animals exhibit, describes a chance encounter with—of all organisms—a weasel. Within the context of a meeting between Dillard and the weasel, Dillard notes how the weasel has a single mindset, only concerned for its sustenance, compared to modern day society that is obsessed with the newest technology and procuring of superficial goods unnecessary for survival. (This is a perfect example of why women and environmentalists should not be allowed to run businesses. If these types of people were left to dictate the demands of corporations, manage national economics, and enact policies, why, they would even resist my decision to lay off the factory workers! Honestly, these people lack common sense. If I was to continue the employment at my factory, how could I automate local production with machines? And more importantly, how could I justify the purchase of my new smartphone, if production were to be still run be humans and not programmable machines?)

In a similar (and still unfounded) point, Thoreau claims that humanity should focus on "simplicity" and "only necessity." Thoreau's argument, while essentially the same as Dillard's argument, defines more clearly how, in the terms of Transcendentalism, living only by necessity is achieved. According to Thoreau, the ultimate life is one that is lived "fully awake." Continuing on with Thoreau's thesis, the reader finds that, to be fully awake, a man must become educated in worldly ideas and principles, yet be concerned with only living for the desire of truth, much like the way Dillard's weasel only lives to survive (I find this as proof that I made the right choice of going to Wharton's rather than some liberal arts school. Imagine, only worrying about thought and logic never having more than just what is needed to survive. I cannot live without my Dreamliner. She has, in retrospect, become a part of my basic level of sustenance. Without her, I would not be able to make any of my international meetings. In fact, I would never have been able to make the flight across the Atlantic in the first place).

Yet while analyzing these two essays, the reader notices how the two authors have differences in their descriptions of transcendentalism. Thoreau (I tell you, the man must have been insane), to demonstrate the tenants of transcendentalism and to live with the utmost conviction, actually resided in a wood for an extended period of time. In the wood, he aspired to live with a heightened sense of meaning and to contribute additional thought and questioning to the intellectual society, goals he felt were of the utmost importance for humanity (Evidently, this guy was not a fund manager. How could sitting next to a pond be more important than the duties of a CFA? Thoreau, rather than generate his own wealth and fixed income for society's elite who, for their entire lives, have worked diligently to procure deserved, fabulous wealth, sat about in the wilderness, likely consuming more than his allotted share of natural resources that would be distributed to him in a world concerned with equality). Dillard, by contrast, merely visited a forested area by her dwelling to experience natural phenomena. Because Dillard lives in a modern society, a society where interconnectedness is so great and survival depends on the goods and services of others, Dillard's visit to the park is more likely for someone of her day and age and is more relatable to her audience. Readers could understand Dillard's sudden surprise when she spots a weasel, since she is unaccustomed to the wild animal, despite being in a natural setting.

Essentially, the tone, diction, and mood of both essays are intentionally created so that readers in the respective eras would be able to grasp the meaning underlying Transcendentalism. Thoreau (a dull New England man of the dull 1800s), wrote to an elite group of thinkers well versed in classical knowledge. His wide use of allusions and puns, which included, "There comes a season in every man's life . . . " was to appeal to scholars who understood the meaning behind the allusions and would find the puns witty and insightful. As the majority of the population of Thoreau's era received a minimal education, Thoreau was unconcerned about the common man grasping his ideals or deciding to follow his philosophy. Instead, Thoreau believed that his education and enlightened ideals of transcendentalism should guide the common man. Additionally, Thoreau may even have believed the common person of the era would not have the intellectual capacity to understand philosophy of any sort. Dillard's essay, by contrast, utilizes language in a manner easily accessible to a reader of the modern era. The diction Dillard uses, unlike her concepts, is straightforward and ready to be read by anyone. In keeping, Dillard sparingly used puns and allusions, aware that a portion of potential readers may not understand a pun while other readers may become confused at the insertion of an allusion, a result of the broad and nearly universal public education system within America. Dillard also uses rhythmic language within her essay instead of traditional prose, possibly an attempt to create a more enjoyable experience for the readers (I find, regardless of what the experts say, that both writing styles are really annoying. I mean, here Thoreau is, trying to be intellectual, and he constantly refers to Chinese gods and Greek Vedas. The religions he mentioned are all false which makes his arguments inaccurate. He clearly never took a finance class; Thoreau constantly turns down offers to make a profit, only further decreasing his worth as a person. And Dillard is none the better; Dillard, instead of using her time wisely by looking over income statements or cash flows of, oh, maybe GEO or PRFDX, she wastes her time playing with weasels and walking outside. Hopefully, her husband has enough fiscal sense and Financial Fitness to take care of the both of them).

It is hard in a world exhibiting a high level of interdependencies, to find novel ways of living. Annie Dillard and David Thoreau, authors living in two different centuries, use their skills as logicians and writers to explore the philosophy of transcendentalism, in the process exploring different ways of living one's life (of course with all the time they put into thinking about life, they must have forgotten their financial planning. If all they ever thought about was how to live, how did they plan for what to do after they died? I'm sure there's a sad story about Thoreau's family being forced to pay outrageous fees after he was deceased because he failed to buy an appropriate life insurance policy. I think these two writers should have been more concerned about the important things like what happened to their money after they were legally deceased). Excerpts from *Living Like Weasels* and *Walden* offer perspectives of lifestyles. We must, in order to be considered fully "awake," analyze our lifestyles to determine the best way to live (which should include monitoring of ETF's for an optimal fiscal return).
With utmost regards,
W. Street

SUMMARY NOTES

Parody appears relatively easy at first to students who start with imitation, but they quickly discover the challenges involved in the form. The irony and subsequent humor created by the form intrigues students, however, and they are more likely to spend a longer time working and reworking their rhetoric.

9

Applications with Musings and Journaling

British novelist and essayist Virginia Woolf once referred to the material in her journals as "this loose, drifting material of life."[1] Many English teachers use student journaling as a focusing activity, but it can be so much more, a place to capture and consider all of that "loose, drifting material." Journals introduced across the curriculum would serve our students' development as writers. The time needed to allow journaling in every class could be minimal, yet the results should be immense.

American writer Flannery O'Connor said of the journal entry: "The longer you look at one object, the more of the world you see in it."[2] Teaching our students to be thoughtfully observant is a valuable skill for any type of academic endeavor. Keeping journals and allowing for illustrations in addition to text gives students creative control over their responses, as well as engages them.

To make the journal most effective in helping young writers develop, however, teachers and parents need to allow for choice in topics. The temptation is for the teacher or parent to provide the topic, and that action defeats part of the value of journaling. The length of a journal entry, likewise, needs to be student initiated. A few pithy lines are more valuable than two pages of repetitive language.

In his collective work as writer and editor of *An Illustrated Life*, Danny Gregory shares writers' words about the value of keeping journals:

- "My journal helps me remain sensitive to my surroundings. . . . It is also grounding because of the quiet concentration," wrote Rick Beerhorst.

- "A sketchbook is a great, nonthreatening place to begin to draw. It also turned out to be an ideal place to develop ideas."
- "My sketchbooks are junk drawers filled with odds and ends: AA batteries, twisty ties, and bad poetry," stated Bill Brown.
- "French architect Eugene Viollet-le-Duc said to consider drawing as a language, like writing, and as a tool to investigate and represent things," added Simonetta Capecchi.[3]

One of the most freely flowing forms of writing is the musing. It is difficult to master because the tendency is to lose the thematic thread holding it loosely together. The genre may also scare some teachers and students because we're not sure where it will lead, but that is also its beauty and contribution to writing. The form may take the writer to unexpected places, offering puzzles to be solved and presenting ideas that had not previously been considered. The musing works well when we want students to brainstorm a topic and become explorers in the continent of a particular subject matter.

Michael*
Critters on the Chain
I'm sitting in my basement, trying to figure out what to write. My eyes hurt because it's 3:00 AM, and I've been doing history homework for the past two hours. The pain is distracting me. I can also hear noises upstairs. This makes me nervous. I'm not supposed to be up at 3:00 AM! Assuming it's a parent, I turn off a few lights and get ready to fake sleeping. Suddenly, I realize that it isn't one of my parents. The noise is zooming down the stairs much faster than either of my parents could move at this hour. I look up from my laptop and discover the source—Sasha.

Sasha is our cat. Originally my sister's, and now that she's off to college, it's up to us to take care of her. Well . . . it's up to my parents. I'm not too good with pet maintenance. Sasha still took a liking to me, though.

Normally, I'd sigh and keep working. However, this time, Sasha had something, something in her teeth. I squint. I lean forward. And suddenly I'm even more panicked than when I thought Sasha was my mother upstairs. *A mouse?!*

Sasha is an indoor cat! How did she catch a mouse? Do we have mice in our house? What do I do? Do I congratulate her? Do I scold her? Do I try to save the mouse? What would happen then? What would happen to it if I didn't? Would Sasha actually try to eat it? Will she leave it somewhere where we'd find it unexpectedly? Why did she come here with it? She does this with socks sometimes . . . then she offers it as a gift . . . it's so *ADORABLE* with socks, but this? What's she doing now? Is she going to drop it? Not in front of me! I like mice! We used to have two mice as pets! I don't know how many stuffed mice I've befriended during my childhood . . . but the same goes for cats! *WHAT?!* It's getting away from her! That crumpled mouse is alive!? It's coming towards me! I pick up my feet, but Sasha grabs the mouse before it can escape by more than six inches.

So she ran off with the mouse, over to the underside of the stairs. I feel enormous guilt for not doing anything as I hear high squeaks from a mouse putting up a good fight. What could I have done? Woken my parents? They'd have been upset. They'd probably even want to kill it!

So I sit here and decide to write about what just occurred before my eyes. And just as I'm scribbling on this page, I see another tiny creature scamper behind an overhead light panel through the ceiling tiles. I wonder how many more there are!

Thus, I go to bed thinking about nature's rightful food chain while forcibly ignoring the notion that my ceiling tile rodent might have liked the former specimen.

Catherine* wrote the following composition for another class but submitted it to me for publication. Her teacher also strongly encouraged creative techniques in applications of writing assignments. She later took AP English with me, and I noticed that her skills continued to grow with the creative risks she took in her academic writing.

Catherine
Call Me Ishmael

I remember the day exactly. It was my first class: philosophy. Patiently I sat, with my books ready on my desk, as I stared at the whiteboard ahead, listening to the commotion surrounding me. Voices of students in the hall could be heard as they scattered into their classrooms, while inside the anticipation of the substitute teacher forced everyone to their seats. The door to our room opened slowly as it revealed our substitute. He was massive, built mostly of muscle and fur, a creature known to all of us as one found in zoos. Our teacher was a gorilla?

"I'm Ishmael," he said while clearing his throat, like a Melville character coming onshore. After the initial shock of hearing him speak, I chuckled to release my tingling nerves. Our first lesson, as we would learn, was on culture. Ishmael posed a question on the board, "With man gone, will there be hope for gorilla?" It seemed simple: gorilla had lived without man before; clearly they could do so now. But Ishmael was not satisfied. Slipping into meditation, my thoughts became clearer. I envied the life of the gorilla. Reminiscing on thoughts of Thoreau and Dillard, I wondered how it felt to live a simple life. To have time as merely a muse, my opportunities seemed endless. The grades I earned had always been important to me, but no matter the education I was getting what knowledge I took from it became essential. Longing to know the difference between truth and ignorance, I questioned everything I learned. No longer accepting things for how they were, I became knowledgeable about common beliefs. I wanted to separate my material ideas from my survival instincts. This simple idea of course came so easily to the gorilla standing in front of me.

> Sinking further into thought, I felt captured by Ishmael's wisdom, Quinn's creation. I began to cherish my life's necessities. In order to be like a new born child, innocent of cultural beliefs, I spent time freeing myself from propaganda. However, only realizing it always follows. I read as much as I could get my hands on. This question became like a math equation, and I wouldn't stop trying to solve it until I got the answer right. Gorillas live a life with the common knowledge of how to survive. They grow up, they mate, they have families, and they provide them with food and shelter. The basic life pattern I hoped to someday obtain was easily accessible to the gorilla.
>
> So it was then that I began to wonder. Maybe we weren't so different from gorillas anyway? What if the gorilla way of life was one for which we all secretly longed for? It became clear to me; I solved the equation: without man, gorilla would survive. However, "with gorilla gone, will there be hope for man?"

In his article "Unspoken Truths" for *Vanity Fair*, Christopher Hitchens wrote, "To my writing classes I used later to open by saying that anybody who could talk could also write."[4] Yet we spend years teaching our students how to write in a way that is dramatically removed from their everyday speech. Both the journal and the musing offer forms that more closely capture that natural voice and are therefore genres that our students feel more comfortable in exploring.

Bruce Pirie suggests the value of asking students to write a musing or another less restrictive form of response: this type of writing helps students arrive at exactly what it is they are thinking and offers ways for them to examine possible themes as well as thesis. "Certainly there is little justification for telling students to decide on a thesis before they start writing: this effectively precludes the possibility of learning through the writing."[5]

10

◎

Applications with Unusual Vessels and Technology

SECTION 1: STUDENT APPLICATIONS WITH UNUSUAL VESSELS

For a character study on Toni Morrison's *Song of Solomon*, students were encouraged to experiment with creative choice in their approaches to character analysis. Although a number of students wrote traditional, analytical papers in which they discussed the seeming paradoxes of character traits, one student chose to create a medical diagnosis. This student was simultaneously taking a course in psychology, allowing him to explore cross-curricular concepts with tremendous success. After he shared his medical paper with the class, we had one of our best class discussions on the nature of man.

Admittedly, allowing students this freedom of choice in designing or creating a container for their ideas can be intimidating, even daunting for the teacher. When one young man submitted his analytical character study in the form of a musical composition with an annotated guide, I was surprised and a little unnerved. I had to discuss the musical aspects of the piece with a music teacher. The mood and tone of the student's work were interpretable and accurately reflected the character of Guitar from Toni's Morrison's novel *Song of Solomon*. While I am very glad that I gave him this creative freedom, I did alter my rubric to make sure that the final product was a written composition since the goal of my class was to improve my students' writing. I will never forget the composition, however, and I knew that he had analyzed the character with tremendous thoughtfulness. Here is the sheet that he handed in along with a CD of his original musical composition.

Bill*
Guitar's Plight: Character Study from Toni Morrison's *Song of Solomon*

I. Instrumentation

Brass	
8 Horn in F—Treble Clef	Horn in F—Bass Clef
3 Trumpet in B♭	2 Trombone
Reeds	
2 Alto Flute	2 Flute
2 Piccolo	2 Contra-bassoon
4 Bassoon	2 Bass Clarinet
3 Oboe	3 English Horn
Strings	
1 Orchestral Harp	8 Violin
4 Viola	4 Cello
4 Bass	
Percussion	
1 Timpani	
Choir	
Bass	Alto
Soprano	Tenor
II. Notes—Key of E♭ major	Common Time

Bill's interpretation of Guitar revealed the character's stridency, yet the musical composition also showed Morrison's character's sensitive side punctuated with his murderous streak and violence. I felt each of the character's opposing tensions in Bill's music in a way I might not have experienced them in prose. Even if this student had failed to fully capture the paradoxes in Morrison's book, he was successful in thinking deeply about Guitar and considering his individuality as well as what he symbolized in the novel. Admittedly, this approach offered very little in terms of writing, yet I found that the creative project had tremendous value for the student and certainly involved a deep level of critical thinking (as well as furthering his musical career).

Anecdotally, this student went on to Rider University, performed at Carnegie Music Hall, and wrote to me later to express gratitude for the creative freedom he was given in our English class. He added that it helped him immensely in his studies throughout and after secondary school.

This student chose a creative form to best fit his concepts, not a concept to force into a predetermined form.

SUMMARY NOTES

Allowing students to choose a form to fit the content rather than the other way around has the advantage of deeply engaging students, leading them to think critically and creatively about texts as well as their responses.

SECTION 2: STUDENT APPLICATIONS WITH TECHNOLOGY: USING WHAT THEY LOVE

Texting

When we look around our classrooms and see our students texting fluently with their various forms of electronic devices, particularly their cell phones, we are frustrated that this engagement does not seem to transfer to academic writing. Yet there are ways to incorporate their love of technology into the writing curriculum, building upon what fascinates them instead of working against it. They are already breaking the rules creatively; we need to find ways to create that balance with creative outlet and academic structures. In a lesson in our *Hamlet* and language play unit, I recently built in a texting application and found that the engagement, critical thinking, and dialogue were deeper and richer during and after the lesson. I have included that activity and student task here as an example of how technology can be incorporated into the lesson.

Texting Hamlet Task: *Hamlet* is a tragedy that is rich in the language of ambiguity and miscommunication, either deliberate or unintentional, between the characters. Hamlet's liberal use of puns and double entendres is designed to confuse the receiver of his messages. For this project, imagine you are a contemporary Hamlet or Ophelia or Claudius or Gertrude . . . you get the idea. Now, you will text a message to another character. You may, of course, use puns. Remember, texting does not allow for innuendo or tonal changes to indicate sarcasm . . . it's all done with language. Imagine Ophelia pondering Hamlet's text message, reading simply, "?" Is Hamlet suggesting that he does not understand Ophelia's message, which she might interpret as mocking her since Hamlet is obviously intellectually sharper than his ladylove? Is Claudius's text to Hamlet, "LOL," meant to mean that he thinks Hamlet is funny as in "to be mocked"? After playing with the language of texting, consider how it might be used against someone or to mock him or her.

Procedures:

1. Take out your cell phone. Yes, that's right! The one you usually have in your pocket anyway.

2. Select a name of the character you will portray in our language and communication "experiment."
3. After selecting your character, think about how your character acts, responds, and relates to others in the play. You have to know the play!
4. On the whiteboard, write your cell phone number next to the character you are portraying.
5. Begin texting one another while remaining in character. See what messages turn up, and consider how you interpret them.
6. Any messages that you are not sure of how to interpret should be written down on a separate sheet of paper. We will keep track of these ambiguous messages and discuss what they might mean as a whole class after our texting activity.
7. Take notes as you text in preparation for our class discussion.

Activity Assessment:
- Engaged texting in character and notes by number of texts
- Class discussion on the ambiguities of language

Assignment and Assessment: You will write a four-page essay on the deliberate ambiguities of Shakespeare's language as compared to the ambiguities discovered in the language of texting.

In this activity, students are taking risks and playing with tone as well as characterization interpretation. They are thinking critically about how characters interact and how language can be both interpreted and misinterpreted. Although the texting they do for the lesson does not equate to an analytical paper about Shakespeare's language play, it can be used to help them think critically about language and character.

Blogging

In my AP English Literature and Composition class, I noticed that a few students dominated the conversation even in our Socratic Circle dialogues. There was an intimidation factor at work that even the best classroom strategies could not entirely overcome. When we began our blogging activity, however, I found that many of the quiet students became our most active bloggers. Unfettered by the length of time it takes to form their rhetoric, they were free to contribute to the discussion. The blogging resulted in some very creative responses that indicate a deeper level of critical thinking than we typically find in a class discussion in which students have a more limited time frame in which to respond.

Ben*
I agree with Laura's point of view; however, I feel as though there is more to the lack of question marks within Benjy's narrative. Faulkner leaves out this specific form of punctuation not only because Benjy can not differenti-

ate between questions and statements, but because he has no social voice. During this period of time, autistic or other mentally ill people were looked upon with apprehension because nobody truly understood the condition. Therefore the autistic portion of society did not have the ability to make their own decisions or speak out against their own abuse. Benjy's narrative lacks question marks because every question asked of him is blatantly rhetorical; he has the potential to answer these questions but the time period in which he lives restrains his progress and ability to contribute to his surroundings. With this misuse of punctuation, Faulkner attempts to give a voice to those in society who have been silenced.

Sarah*

I know this seems odd for this topic, but I wonder if Quentin (man) had any sort of close relationship with Dilsey. I mean I don't remember her being brought up in his section, which makes his unique because in the three other narratives, she plays a pivotal role. I don't think that just because Quentin is not around Dilsey at the time of Quentin's narrative excludes her, because he speaks of all of his own family. He really doesn't mention the help at all in his section, probably because he had his father looking out for him; a benefit which none of the other children received during their upbringing (page 76). I wish I could find out Quentin's opinion on the help, because they were obviously around and keeping the Compson family together as best as they possibly could. Does anyone else remember anything significant from Quentin's section about Dilsey? Because unlike every other character, she seems not to be present in Quentin's narrative.

Christine*

Ok, so I may not be able to find any citations, but I think it's still an intriguing point. I believe that Kurtz represents society; he is a one-man empire, similar to Milo in *Catch-22*. Similar to large empires like Rome, Egypt, and many others, Kurtz came from a small beginning. He started out being just a steamboat captain, and he charmed the natives and his employers. He quickly rose to a position of legendary status, as he was quite good at his job. He gathered more ivory than people thought was possible. But the Congo got to him. He randomly beheaded people, because that was his skewed perspective of cannibalism. By the end of the novel, Kurtz has practically withered away to nothing by the time Marlow gets there to see him. The manager tells Kurtz that the company no longer wants him, because he is too risky. After that, Kurtz simply shrivels up and dies. This is very similar to the rise and fall of great empires. I think Kurtz shows what happens to all great European things when they get too large and out of control.

Patrick*

Yes, because Benjy seems to have a form of autism, Faulkner portrays Benjy as having the inability or desire to manipulate or deceive. Rather than examining what a thought or action may allow him to gain, Benjy describes scenarios as he interprets them. Case in point, the quotation, "Quentin and Luster were playing in the dirt in the front of T.P.'s. There was a fire in the house, rising and falling, with Roskus sitting black in front of it," (31) describes Benjy's plain language and metaphorical use of words to center the situation around fire, the object he understands.

Therefore Benjy, because he narrates events as he interprets them and does not misconstrue details intentionally as opposed to Jason and other family members, he allows the reader an unbiased account of his experiences. Nonetheless, Benjy, despite relaying a truthful perspective of Caddy, cannot have a full understanding of who Caddy is. Rather, because he is a single person and because of his autistic impairments, trusting his thoughts of Caddy as being definitive and infallible will lead to an inaccurate portrayal of Caddy as a complete character.

By contrast, Benjy seems to have an omniscient type of understanding of Caddy through his sense of smell. While still young, Benjy claims that, "Cady smells like trees," signifying her innocence while he notices her scent gradually changes to the smells of perfumes as she matures. Regardless, Benjy only interacts with Caddy's mothering persona, not her promiscuous side. Throughout the text Benjy recalls Caddy comforting him, including the time when, "Caddy held me (Benjy) and I could hear us all, and the darkness," (75) clearly reflecting her motherly instincts.

Because of the complexity contained within a character, a single perspective is often not sufficient to the understanding of who that person is. Faulkner, ever driven to capture a more precise portrait of life, portrays the character Caddy through many lenses and opinions.

Anne Marie*

As we read Jason's section of the novel, we find that he worries so much about what everyone thinks of him and his family. We find what he thinks of Caddy right from the start of his section. "I says she ought to be down there in the kitchen right now, instead of up there in her room . . . " (Faulkner 180). Jason is constantly angry at Caddy and even goes as far as stealing money from her even though she has a family to support. Jason cannot even look at her without getting disgusted. He says, "She hadn't got around to painting herself yet and her face looked like she had polished it with a gun rag," (Faulkner 184). This loathing he has for Caddy seems to come out of no where as all she did was try to keep the family together, and showed more love than anyone else in that family. Now we know that Jason believes we as the reader should feel sorry for him and that he should have been the one to save the family. My question is, why is he so worried about being "normal"? He constantly thinks no one in his family meets the social norms that are established in their home town. This causes him to get angry and he takes that anger out on everyone else, mainly Caddy. If he stopped worrying about everyone else's opinion, could he possibly let go of his anger and try to actually help his family, or is he forever doomed to paranoia by everyone around him?

Tim*

Although I do understand everyone's argument, I feel that Benjy is not actually telling us what he understands. I lean more towards the idea that Benjy is simply recalling or re-experiencing the events and relaying them to the readers. Benjy does not seem able to comprehend what happens to him, the only abstract idea he is vaguely able to understand is sadness and love. He appears unbiased with characters such as Jason and Quentin. Benjy does seem to hold Caddy, however, in a different light. The imagery used to describe her is always more detailed, like her hair being fire. Benjy also seems able to understand pain and suffering. The one emotion that translates is crying. On page 57 is one of the many instances in which Benjy responds by crying. He is unbiased toward Jason and Quentin; however, he seems to view Caddy with a slight distortion of reality.

Kelly*
I agree that Jason does care a little more than he should about appearances, but I also believe that that frame of mind fit the time period accordingly. Also, Jason is furious with Caddy because she took away his only opportunity for a good job at the bank when she ended the marriage between her and Herbert Head. Now, he is angry and stuck at a low income, low class job. He is also the baby of the family (excluding Benjy, but I don't believe Jason really thinks of Ben as a brother as much as he does a burden), and so he is used to having to fight for any attention that he got. He did so by tattling on Caddy whenever she did something wrong, such as on page 39, "I'm going to tell on her too." This tattling created a sort of attention that Jason thrived on, and I believe that, in order to maintain that "near-perfect-child" persona he had with his parents, he tried his hardest to stay out of trouble, so that the tattling was not being done on him. And yes, I do believe that his paranoia will be his downfall, in his personal and business life. He cannot continue, or start to, advance in life if he maintains his angry-at-the-world view, and, of course, he never "advances."

An additional benefit of the writing for the blogs is that students who did not typically interact in a classroom were suddenly communicating and arguing with each other about the text. The connections made through blogging seemed to carry over into the class, and new channels of communication were opened. The blog presented a safe place to express ideas, particularly controversial ones. Perhaps most important, all students participated in the blogging conversations, whereas in a typical classroom, some students talk much more and others are nearly silent. There is simply a higher level of involvement on the part of all of the students.

SUMMARY NOTES

The student writing that is included in these sections demonstrates self-directed, creative choice and creative technique applications of analytical writing. They may be used to model for other students, to initiate class discussions, or to exemplify how a particular creative vehicle may effectively contain an argument.

11

Traditional-Looking Essays Incorporating Creative Techniques

Of course, college requirements demand that we teach academic writing in its most recognizable structures, but that writing need not be staid or boring. And clearly, students know the paragraph essay form very well. They do not need to "practice" it on every writing assignment. Once a student has experimented with the application of creative techniques and creative formats in writing, that student is better able to incorporate those techniques within stricter confines and the immediately recognizable formal structure of the academic essay. In fact, some of the most outstanding papers I have received were written in traditional structures but show perceptive analysis and language versatility indicating the freedom they had experienced. Students were more willing to try creative writing techniques within their academic writing as a result of their earlier creative writing experiences.

This section of student writing may be highly interesting to many educators, as it represents excellent student writing in the most recognizable structure, but each essay shows evidence of rich creativity and student ownership of the writing. These essays were written later in the semester, after students had been given opportunities to explore creative choice and creative techniques. The students found that they were then able to employ the techniques at will to emphasize and strengthen their arguments. Many students wrote about the fact that the instruction in creative techniques and creative choice empowered them and made them self-identify as writers and scholars.

Sam*

A Pun Palooza

Daunting, brilliant, and complex are all words that could easily be used to describe Shakespeare's word play. Shakespeare uses words like an architect would use mere materials to construct an elaborate cathedral. Sure, there is literal meaning at every turn, but there is also a complex underground lattice of hidden meaning. Shakespeare uses words to construct lines that may contain two or more distinct meanings. The purpose of a cathedral is to worship God, while Shakespeare's purpose is to write a tragedy; different as they are, the parallels are striking. The hidden symbols carved into the walls of the cathedral are akin to Shakespeare's puns. Moreover, Shakespeare's use of the English language to create a work that is poetic at times is like how the cathedral has an innate beauty. In all likelihood, there is no easy answer to why Shakespeare would write in this elaborate style. That being said, his puns certainly add homage to his motifs of revenge and a lack of certainty.

Hamlet's first lines are a perfect example of how Shakespeare's punning underscores both of the aforementioned motifs. Hamlet says, "A little more than kin and less than kind . . . Not so, my lord; I am too much in the sun" (Shakespeare 25). Hamlet is saying that he does not like Claudius. Kind is one word that is a pun. Kind can be benevolent, or something of a similar type. From this pun, Hamlet shows that he dislikes Claudius despite their relationship, by calling him less than kind or nice. When Hamlet says he is too much in the sun, this is a pun on son. Hamlet is saying his close relation to Claudius is the cause of his discontent. Just Hamlet's first two lines show how rich his language is in hidden meaning. Hamlet's puns give a window into his opinions that otherwise could not be attained. Hamlet can't subtly say he loathes the king without him hearing. Instead, his puns allow him this luxury. This allows the audience to understand what is going on in Hamlet's head. Understanding Hamlet is key to grasping the motifs of revenge and uncertainty. Already, the seeds have been planted for Hamlet's desire for revenge. He detests the king even before he knows that Claudius killed his father. This pun will later allow the audience to understand the scope of Hamlet's desire for revenge. In terms of a lack of certainty, Hamlet constantly grapples with this idea. When the reader isn't sure in what way to take Hamlet's speech, this inability to achieve certainty becomes painfully obvious. Through this, the motif of uncertainty is passed to the audience. The puns in these lines set the stage for all the conflict in the play.

Hamlet's first soliloquy has several examples of word play that accentuate Hamlet's inner struggle about his mother marrying Claudius. The first line in the soliloquy is, "O, that this too, too, sullied flesh would melt, Thaw and resolve itself into a dew . . . " (Shakespeare 29). This word play is extremely clever. The words resolve and dew imply action. Through Hamlet's punning, the reader can understand his inner turmoil. Hamlet wants so badly, to act, to seek revenge, but can't bring himself to do it. Later in the soliloquy, Hamlet says, "'Tis an unweeded garden that grows to seed, Things rank and gross in nature . . . " (Shakespeare 29). Again there is a pun in these lines. The unweeded garden is a symbol for Denmark's current state. Unweeded could imply that there are errands to be done or there are problems within the government. Denmark being unweeded, could be a symbol that Hamlet needs to kill Claudius for his treachery. It could also mean that the entire country is in disarray. Hamlet saying things are rank and gross in nature is another double pun. Rank can mean status or stench and gross can mean an amount or disgusting. In other words, he is insulting the king and at the same time calling the death of his father gross. The motif of a lack of certainty is clearly within these lines. Hamlet does not know what to do. He is not sure of his actions. At the same time, he is driven to revenge. At this point, Hamlet does not know that Claudius murdered his father. Therefore, these puns are not for Hamlet's use, but for the audience's understanding. From this, it is obvious that Shakespeare also uses puns for the audience's benefit.

The scene is rife with puns. One of the most important ones is found when Hamlet is talking with Claudius. Hamlet says, "Excellent, I' faith of the chameleon's. I eat the air, promise-crammed" (Shakespeare 141). This is a pun on the word air. In Shakespeare's day, chameleons were thought to live on air (Folger's Library 140). The pun here is that Hamlet really means the word "heir." He essentially tells Claudius that he eagerly awaits to be heir, on Claudius's promises. This really contributes to the motif of uncertainty. The audience can only wonder what goes on in Claudius's head when Hamlet makes this comment. He probably intuited the meaning but did not want to believe it or questioned himself. Thus, this pun again blurs the line between uncertainty and reality. In terms of revenge, Hamlet is telling the audience watching the play that he lives off the idea of revenge and power. With revenge he will take the crown. Therefore, this pun shines a light on the fact that Hamlet wants revenge. When he says the only food he lives on is air, it shows that revenge has consumed him. Because of this, the motif is underscored by this pun.

Uncertainty is probably always on the mind of Claudius. He does not know what to think about Hamlet's puns and hinting. The play convinced Claudius that Hamlet was a threat. Throughout the play, but after this scene in particular, he uses the word madness to describe Hamlet's state. He says, "I like him not, nor stands it safe with us / To let his madness range" (Shakespeare 163). Madness is a brilliant and ever-appropriate pun. Madness can mean anger or insanity. Hamlet is feigning insanity because he is angry. Thus, Claudius saying he will not let Hamlet's madness range is a pun. Range also sounds very similarly to rage. Madness raging would describe the level of Hamlet's anger. Again this pun is used throughout the play. It reinforces the motif of uncertainty. The audience is left to ponder whether Claudius means anger or Hamlet's insanity. When the audience is faced with a similar problem as the main character, a greater understanding of the motif is attained. When we interpret madness to mean anger, it underscores the motif of revenge. It is ironic that Claudius does not want Hamlet's "madness" to go unchecked because presumably he is using insanity as the definition for madness. Hamlet is so angry for revenge, that it consumes all of him; this is a central theme: revenge can be all consuming.

Another example of a language play is found when Hamlet confronts Gertrude in bedroom. Gertrude says, "Hamlet, thou hast thy father much offended" (Shakespeare 169). In response, Hamlet says, "Mother, thou hast my father much offended" (Shakespeare 169). This play on words is very important to both the motifs of not knowing what is certain and the all-consuming nature that revenge has. Hamlet's mother tells Hamlet that he has offended Claudius, using the word father. Hamlet turns this around on her and says that she has offended his real father. The pun here is in the word father. Father can literally mean father, or in Gertrude's context a person that more or less assumes the role as a father. Hamlet finally tells his mother how he feels about her and Claudius being married. Uncertainty comes into play here when the audience and Gertrude expect Hamlet to answer Gertrude's prompt in regard to Claudius. Hamlet's turnaround is surprising and the opposite what is expected. Therefore, certainty is thrown into question. This pun underscores the fact that we can never know what will happen next; we can never know a person's next move. This pun also is linked to the motif of revenge because it highlights one of the reasons Hamlet wants to kill Claudius: he married Hamlet's mother. Hamlet is so obsessed with this that he is thinking about it even when Gertrude asks an unrelated question. This shows the intensity of Hamlet's drive for revenge. For such a simple exchange, there is a great deal of significance to it.

More examples of word play are found when Hamlet is talking with the gravedigger. When asked how the gravedigger heard Hamlet became mad, he says, "Very strangely, they say" (Shakespeare 249). Here the pun is on the word *strangely*. Strange can mean *strange*, as in weird, or *strange*, as in suspicious. The gravedigger probably means that Hamlet became mad in a strange way in terms of its weirdness. However, the audience can catch the dramatic irony in the pun. Hamlet becomes angry because of how Claudius killed King Hamlet, suspiciously. The strange circumstances surrounding Hamlet's father's death is ultimately why Hamlet seeks revenge. Again, revenge is appropriate to discuss. Even more germane to this pun is the motif of never being able to be certain of anything. The grave digger does not know why Hamlet became mad, only that it was through "strange happenings." He is uncertain about the exact causes. No one can be certain a rumor is true without confirmation. Therefore, again this motif becomes relevant.

A final example of a pun that demonstrates the motifs of revenge and uncertainty is found when Hamlet is talking with Laertes at the fencing match. He borrows the same pun used so often by Claudius. Hamlet says, "Who does it, then? His madness. If't be so, Hamlet is the faction that is wronged; His madness is poor Hamlet's enemy" (Shakespeare 273). This pun ties together the entire play. Hamlet uses the same pun Claudius does, with the same meanings of madness. It is interesting that Hamlet says his own madness is his enemy. This may be true in many senses. In terms of the lack of certainty motif, it is present here as well. One would think that Hamlet is responsible for his own actions, but he says this is not the case. This contrasts between logic and what seems to be certain which creates uncertainty as it is, more or less, the opposite of what is expected. When revenge consumes someone it is not a good happening. Hamlet says that revenge is his enemy here which adds more substance to the theme that revenge is all-consuming. When revenge is this all-consuming, it becomes an enemy to the person seeking revenge as Hamlet states. This line summarizes the whole play if imagination is used. This play is all about Hamlet seeking revenge, and how this seeking of revenge leads to Hamlet's tragic downfall. Revenge coupled with his proclivity to think situations out are Hamlet's tragic flaws that lead to his demise.

Shakespeare's use of puns and language play is one of the reasons that he is still so widely read today. Reading Shakespeare is like reading a puzzle. Lines must be broken down, words must be looked up, and syntax changes must be reordered. Still, when all said and done, if one can decipher a work of Shakespeare there is an incredible reward. In this play, Shakespeare's word play is not only to keep his audience interested, but to let the audience understand how the characters are feeling. The motifs of revenge and uncertainty are hidden within these puns. In the end, *Hamlet* has a riveting plot to being with, but it is how Shakespeare uses words that make the literature cross into the extraordinary.

In the following essay, the student analyzes his own creative processes in writing. He wrote the essay while enrolled in a college, but he sent it to me because he wanted to share the ideas and attributed part of his success in the course and in writing to our creative journeys in class during high school.

Jon*

Daftly Building a Castle on a Swamp

As I sat gazing at the bright, eye straining light of my computer screen, I could recall the time some of my acquaintances and I traveled to Madrid after the apocalypse had destroyed human civilization. We stole away in the drearily colored buildings under the non-descript sky, hiding from the horrors of the nuclear fallout, Dave Mustaine, and date rape. My friends Dave and Steve were with me, but this was much before the former took up residence in a cardboard box in the fiery depths of hell and the latter became a much sought after pimp.

Of course, in reality our adventure was undeniably impossible, but with pen, paper, ink, and a smidgen of imagination, my friends and I brought these stories to life. I would confess that the earliest of them must have been atrocious narratives that no one in their right mind would have read. They were filled with obscure inside jokes and internet references that hardly anyone could have understood, but that was beside the point. These stories were not meant for anyone else; they existed for the sole purpose of our enjoyment.

To trace these juvenile stories back to the beginning, they likely started with our politically correct fairytales, such as *Snow White and the Seven Little People*, but became more complex when my friend, Dave, wrote *Apocalypse Please*, which took place in Madrid after Santa Claus had accidentally caused full scale nuclear warfare worldwide. This story, as well as the next few that were written, had become a medium for friendly teasing and personal attacks between our friends, as well as a chance to humorously slight some of our least favorite celebrities, such as the aforementioned Dave Mustaine. To us, these jokes and fairytales were more than just a bit of humor; they allowed us to laugh at ourselves and each other without anyone taking offense. Of course, there were a few spots where things were taken a bit too far, such as when I had to beg Dave, "Can I please not sound like a complete stuttering moron in every single chapter you make?" It never led to any sort of fighting between us, however, as the best way to take revenge on a friend for a particularly bad insult was to put him in a position twice as awkward in another story.

Apocalypse Please, was just the tip of the iceberg, however, as we cranked out more and more of our own stories. In retaliation for his treatment of me, in my story, *Map of the Problematique,* I placed Dave in the protagonist role as a hoboesque loser living in a cardboard box in the scorching depths of hell. Even worse, he was employed as a servant of Satan, who was modeled after myself, and also married unhappily to a girl whom we knew personally. "If you keep me married to Emily or have me end up with Jackie in the end, I'll kill you," Dave jokingly told me, which was a sign that I had hit the sweet spot that would exact my revenge. Between being annoyed by Justin Bieber, Hillary Clinton, and the Jonas Brothers, Dave was tasked with stopping a crusader ninja trying to assassinate hell's most powerful assets. All of this reached a complete breaking point when Elvis was revealed as being god, turning everything on its head once again.

If it sounds childish and terrible, it most definitely was, as were the stories that came after it. My friends and I were, at one point or another, casted as rock stars, set to do Powerthirst commercials, became murderers on a rampage, and every manner of imaginable embarrassing or ridiculous situation imaginable. But that's not what matters. What was important is the way we were writing. Soon, the straight forward he-said-she-said of the politically correct fairy tales became much too tiresome and stiff, which led to the more descriptive later stories. Even they, however, were not complex enough to satisfy us as writers anymore, so we began striving for that next quantum leap forward. Our early images of dark nights and cobblestone streets gave way to scenes of tracks of the today's assorted stagecoaches laced in the quagmires of sloshing muck and mire leftover from the spring's constant rain while the villagers exaggeratedly lifted their feet as they walked to the market and back. The change was immediate and noticeable, and my friends that read it took note. As my friend Steve put ever so eloquently, "I really like your mud!"

Our early narratives consisting of only humorous personal attacks on each other with barely any actual substance served as our bait into the world of storytelling, which we took with the ferocity of a starving bull shark. What kept us on the reel, however, was the desire to be better and better and write things that people beyond our immediate circle of friends could enjoy. That's not to say, however, that we don't include humor anymore, as I was always willing to sneak in a few puns, malapropisms, or humorous references every chance I get, but it's not what the entire narrative is about any longer.

Writing became something deeper for me; it was about creating a world that's real enough to live in, with characters that are either likeable or detestable, or even a little bit of both. It was about creating a story that another person could understand and build upon in their mind. It was about doing the unexpected. I enjoyed surprising the reader at every turn; I could create one small sentence that would appear to be of minimal importance in chapter one, then have the entire fate of the world depend on it by chapter ten. To tell my own story became like playing god in a universe of my own creation. Every character's existence was in my hands, and only I had the power to choose whether to crush them in my grip or open my fist and display them to the entire world.

There still, however, needed to be more. In the same way that my friends and I only knew our jokes and insults were perfect if we made each other squirm a bit in our seats, a story is only worth telling if it can make a person question their beliefs and bring up an idea that they might find uncomfortable. Narratives are the best way to bring up questions of the afterlife, religion, god, love, or anything else that people generally take with a relatively narrow view. For example, I asked my friends at one point, "Who do you think is empirically good or evil, the Christian god or Satan?"

"Of course god is the positive force and Satan is evil. How could it be the other way around?" Was the predictable response that most people came up with. I could sit at my computer all day and make arguments about how Satan's actions could have been interpreted as a positive for humanity, or about how he can represent questioning predetermined authority, or how the bible states that god has killed over 250,000 times more people than Satan, but people will only revert back to their original beliefs when questioned outright. A narrative, however, could be subtle and would allow a controversial or unpopular statement to be made through implication, forcing the reader to take hold of all the perspectives in a given situation. Creating characters in the guise of traditionally accepted forces or entities that are dynamic and progress away from most people's initial interpretations of them was much more effective than any outright argument with someone who was already set on their beliefs.

It was sometimes shocking for me to imagine that simple jokes through storytelling could lead to using narrative to question religion, society, politics, and personal relationships, but, in truth, the process was largely the same. While our earliest attempts at satire were crude and unpolished, they were what laid the groundwork for the complex thoughts and arguments that I could only create with the knowledge gained from my previous failures and inadequate writing.

Most importantly of all, despite my love of forcing people to question their beliefs, I periodically ensured that I did not take myself too seriously. After all, enjoying the writing process and allowing my friends to have fun reading my stories took precedence over all of the smaller factors. In that sense, writing was my personal escape and personal ritual. Whenever something was on my mind, my first reaction was to reach for my trusty Uni-Ball Vision Elite pen and let the dark, flowing ink spill out from my head, through my hand, and onto the stark white paper and hope that the reality of my words exceeds that of the paper I had marred, a worry that I had inherited from Harold Acton.

All of this brought me back to being seated in my room, staring at my words on the computer screen, ideas of cursed gems, the Seraphim, demons, and a continent full of problems to take on flowing through my head, and as I destroyed the traditional cliché of good versus evil, I could not help but reflect on where I have come from. The buildings and settings that went undeveloped and raw on paper were alive inside of me, filled with the menacing cloudy violet and crimson sky overlooking the decrepit and monochromatic image of Madrid, devoid of any life and movement, as well as the darkest depths of hell burning somewhere below that, filled with monstrous abominations. As I came out of my introspection, I could only come to the conclusion that a piece of both worlds were inside the one I was creating now, and maybe, someday, this world would be alive inside of another that will be even more developed, more complex.

Consider writing tasks designed to help students examine a concept and make an argument but do not dictate the form or format.

Sample Task: Stylistically distinctive and publishing their major works approximately 120 years apart, the texts of Henry David Thoreau and Annie Dillard are often paired in terms of their themes, specifically, enlightenment through experience of the natural world. In a roughly five-page, comparison/contrast analysis, address the intertextuality of Thoreau's "Where I Lived, and What I Lived for," the second chapter from *Walden*, and Dillard's "Living Like Weasels," the first work in her book *Teaching a Stone to Talk.* You may want to incorporate their use of the juxtaposition of opposites in addition to their shared motifs and themes. Feel free to be creative in the approach to your analysis but make sure to support your ideas with textual evidence from Thoreau and Dillard.

In the following excerpts of students' writing, the students were given a task that included specifics without the container for their ideas. They were allowed to choose a traditional essay format, of course, but were encouraged to try a creative framework for their argument. The safety net was that the scoring rubric for this assignment did not penalize students for a "failed" experiment if the learning goals were met. According to educator Allison Zmuda, "Our discomfort with failure will never go away entirely. . . . By accepting the inevitability of failure—and the role it plays in ultimate success—students can move from simply going through the motions of a task to becoming fully engaged learners."[1]

The Summative Assessment: Caddy Compson is often described as the focal character in Faulkner's novel *The Sound and The Fury*, yet she is not given a narrative section of the novel like her brothers. Why? What do we know about Caddy's voice through the filters of Benjamin, Quentin, and Jason, as well as the omniscient narrator of April Eighth, 1928? Why is Caddy considered the focal character? Write a five-page analysis in which you explore Caddy's voice in the novel. In order to examine the ways in which we discover Caddy, you will need to consider the distinctive features of narrative sections of the novel, the verisimilitude of the narrative voices, and the unifying aspects of Faulkner's unusual narrative structure. Your essay should arrive at some conclusions about Caddy and her perspective. You are encouraged to try using some creative techniques within the essay structure.

Andrew*
Caddy's Lost Narrative: The Manifestation of Voice and Identity
The essence of identity is based upon the realities of voice. Authors are always seeking to formulate characters to be as realistic and precise as possible, through their own unique narratives. William Faulkner articulates the complexities of voice in *The Sound and the Fury*, through the extensive usage of narrative point of view which are expressed by the children of the Compson family with one exception, Candace. Also known as Caddy, she is arguably the most important figure in the novel as she represents the object of obsession for all three of her siblings including Benjamin, Quentin, and Jason. Faulkner exemplifies Caddy through a dialogic narrative, as she is portrayed in various ways by her siblings and even by an unknown narrator. Interestingly enough, there is not a narrative presented by Caddy as Faulkner chooses not to include her voice within the novel and, as a result we are forced to develop a conclusion relative to the significance of this very complex protagonist. Instead, the reader is left with biased depictions of Caddy by her siblings and unknown narrator. Faulkner indirectly characterizes Caddy to suggest the importance of voice and the importance of maintaining a balanced perspective among the family, in addition to the deeper symbolic conflict about changes in the South. He classifies this novel as a great "failed narrative," yet it is in fact highly sophisticated and based on the true realities of human thought which are expressed thoroughly and distinctly through this unique dialogic narrative.

April 7th 1928 is the date the novel begins, under the narrative of the youngest Compson—Benjamin. Faulkner begins his novel with a central consciousness narrative as Benjy's thoughts are presented in the text; however, Faulkner illustrates anachrony, in terms of structure, which indicate a fragmented structure. This is done deliberately because Benjy is a grown thirty-three year old man who is also mentally handicapped. At first, it is almost improbable to think of a way to enter the mind of an autistic man, and yet Faulkner dives right into this concept that was simply unheard of. As Benjy describes the events around himself, his diction of concrete words and simple sentence length transform the otherwise ordinary scenes into striking imagery. The metaphors created through Faulkner's simple diction illustrate the beauty of difference and the advantage Benjy gains from looking at the world in this fixed internal point of view. To add on to this, Faulkner deliberately begins the novel with Benjy's section because he is the purest filter of the Compsons' story, partially due to his handicap, he gives an unbiased point of view in relation to all the other characters including Caddy. This character lacks any ability for social interaction due to his lack of communication, and on several occasions this leads to some sort of conflict.

As a result, Caddy takes the responsibility to take care of her younger brother because no one else will. His own mother Caroline Compson is quite simply a horrible maternal figure as she is absent as a mother to her children who has no sense of her children's needs. She even treats the mentally disabled Benjy cruelly and selfishly. Through the central consciousness of Benjy, it is clear the Caddy is an affectionate young woman with a headstrong toughness and versatility. Caddy is presented a "voice" that begins to be heard in Benjy's section of the novel as she comforts Benjy when he moans and whimpers, "What is it, Benjy. Tell Caddy. She'll do it. Try," (Faulkner 41). No matter what Benjy does, Caddy always stays with her brother acting like a mother-like figure and helps him interact. She states, "Why, Benjy. Did you find Caddy again. Did you think Caddy had run away," (Faulkner 42–43).

Benjy, although speechless, is able to notice the slightest of changes including the foreseeable demise of the Compson family and Caddy's changing personality. He notes her changing nature through his acute sense of smell. At first she is described as innocent with a sincere aptitude as he notes, "Caddy smelled like trees and like when she says we were asleep," (Faulkner 6). As the novel progresses, Caddy slowly becomes more promiscuous, and Benjy is capable of sensing that as she loses her innocence, he thinks, " . . . I couldn't smell trees anymore and I began to cry," (40). Benjy clings to his early memories of Caddy and refuses to acknowledge the new reality in which the Compsons find themselves. Through this indirect characterization and symbolization, Faulkner suggests that we should examine our perceptions and motives when we face change so that we may greet it with a balanced perspective. This way of looking at the world is aimed specifically towards Caddy who is never granted a voice. The eldest brother Quentin has a different perspective on whom Caddy is and what she represents in terms of the Compson family, as he is quite simply paralyzed with his obsession with Caddy and that leads to his downfall as a Compson.

Hope is the word that is closely associated with Quentin Compson, the eldest son of the Compson family. Quentin feels an unreasonable burden of responsibility to live up to the family's past magnitude and prestige. He is a very intelligent and sensitive young man, but is paralyzed by his obsession with Caddy and his preoccupation with a very traditional Southern code of conduct and morality. Through a direct discourse narrative, Faulkner expresses Quentin's thoughts as though the eighteen-year old had formulated them. Faulkner uniquely presents the antithesis to Benjy's section through Quentin. We note this distinction in poetic level and narrative as well as sentence structure. For example, on June 2nd, 1910 Quentin thinks, "When the shadow of the sash appeared on the curtains it was between seven and eight o'clock and then I was in time again, hearing the watch," (Faulkner 76). The difference in style is almost a complete contrast to Benjy as the diction use is formulated through abstract words and more figurative language while the syntax presented is through consistent repetition of symbols such as shadows. The structure of the sentences becomes lengthier in Quentin's section. These factors play an important role in terms of the verisimilitude of Caddy's voice which is also manifested in this section of the novel.

The father of Quentin, Jason Compson, sells the pasture for the sake of Quentin's future and hoped for success. Unfortunately for the Compson family, Quentin's stopped living in the present. He turned in upon himself—time and the future and the world outside have stopped mattering all that much. He wanted to focus on his past. Because Caddy was the most important person in Quentin's life, he could not help but think about her and think about how the world views her defiance to the moral code. Quentin illogically believes that if he declares that he has committed incest with Caddy, he will be able to protect her. He thinks: "If it could just be a hell beyond that: the clean flame the two of us more than dead. Then you will have only me then only me then the two of us amid the pointing and the horror beyond the clean flame," (Faulkner 116). A confused sexual desire becomes a reflection of Caddy's own consuming desires. She desires to start a relationship with Dalton Ames and quickly becomes pregnant. Her pregnancy, the death knell of the family according to Mrs. Compson serves as the reason for a quick and unhappy "almost marriage." She effectively disappears from the novel as she is excommunicated, so to state, from the House of Compson. Although Caddy calmly agrees with Quentin's false motivation, she inevitably does not accept his offer of salvation, and as a direct result, Quentin is the one who deteriorates. Quentin discovers that he cannot live in both the past and the present at the same time and that is his undoing; Caddy represents the wayward daughter in Quentin's perspective as opposed to the absent mother for Benjy. Caddy's voice or lack thereof leads the readers to presume that Caddy has drastically changed in terms of behavior, and yet she remains the focal point of the novel. Jason is Caddy's other sibling, and he seeks to exploit all of her wrong doings, one way or another.

April 6th, 1928 is the date in which Jason begins his perspective of the Compson family. Faulkner illustrates a fixed internal point of view as well as a first person narrative situation in this section. Like his brothers, Jason is fixated on Caddy, but his obsession is based on bitterness and a desire to get Caddy in trouble. Ironically, the loveless Jason is the only one of the Compson children who receives Mrs. Compson's affection. Yet, Jason is not one to take compliments, as he seemingly takes every comment as an insult and seeks no affection or love from anyone. The direct discourse narrative allows the readers to understand that Jason, unlike Quentin, focuses on the present and future and yet he has no direct ambition or goal. He only seeks to exploit Caddy and her illegitimate daughter Quentin. Faulkner demonstrates other style elements in this section that become more apparent and distinct such as the usage of slang, in terms of diction use and the simplicity of order in

Jason's section of the novel. It is chronological in structure which adds to the various style choices of which Faulkner makes use. The bitterness of Jason's personality is apparent on the first page of section as he states, "Once a bitch always a bitch, what I say," (180). Jason always finds someone else to blame for his own sorry fate.

The fault is mostly pinned upon Caddy. It is Caddy who does not aid him in getting a job at a bank. It is Caddy who sends money to her daughter, not to him. It is Caddy who took the family name and trampled it into the mud, according to the second brother. Jason even extends his hatred of Caddy to women in general. He additionally hates African Americans and Jews, which give an impure representation of the Compson family because of his biased viewpoints on race, family, and society. Caddy is not mentioned frequently in this section of the novel because of Jason's tunnel-like and his emotionless outlook on humanity, exemplified him as a typical Southern male racist.

The final narrative of the novel is an omniscient narrator that follows the character of Dilsey. It is safe to state that Dilsey is one of the only sources of stability in the Compson household, and she may even be the only source of stability as the novel progresses. Faulkner exemplifies Dilsey as a character disconnected from the Compson family, in a sense, because she is not engulfed by the inevitable demise of the family. She is the only character in the text to witness the beginning and the ultimate, foreseeable end of the dysfunctional Compson household. April 8th, 1928 is the final section of *The Sound and the Fury* and Faulkner presents to the readers a third person omniscient narrative following the events of Dilsey, and as a result, we witness the disintegration of the Compson family. In her own words, "I seed de first en de last," (Faulkner 301). These are Dilsey's powerful words stated because she has been put through a lot in terms of responsibility and leadership. We may expect Caddy to narrate the last section, since she is in many ways the most important character in the novel, and the only one of the Compson children who has not had a chance to speak. However, Faulkner seems to narrate this section himself, from a third-person point of view in a neutral omniscience because Caddy is still focalized all throughout the entire novel through a neglected voice.

Denied a voice, Caddie takes the blame for her brother's pain, and we lack an objective account to clarify her character. Faulkner's narrative illustrates the importance of having a voice and how many of us fail to utilize our own. Without a voice, we could all fall into the pit in which Caddy Compson inhabits. Faulkner imbeds this message more deeply into the text through his symbolization of Caddy as the changes taking place in the Deep South after the Civil War. When you deny voice, you limit. Your perspective remains biased and spotty. Faulkner indirectly characterizes Caddy, denying her the opportunity to share her story, in order to illustrate how important it is that we speak up to the world around us. Faulkner explores further into Caddy's metaphorical importance as the symbol of change in the South. The brothers' fundamentally different means of dealing with change equate to an inability to adapt, suggesting that we must seek a dignified, cohesive, spoken perspective when faced with adversity and hardship.

While the next student's essay appears traditional in structure, the writing is very creative with examples of personification—"a pen does not call itself a pen." What is perhaps most impressive is the fact that he wrote it during a timed, in-class writing test in preparation for the AP English examination. The essay reflects his thoughtful and deep understanding of Samuel Beckett's play *Waiting for Godot* as well as the fact that Beckett first wrote his play in French and produced it in Paris.

Solomon*
Il n'y a pas Godot
Samuel Beckett's play *Waiting for Godot* seems nonsensical. The fact of the matter, though, is that it should be absurd. Not only does the removal of a play's traditional structure help to accentuate the message of the play, but the resulting nonsense is in itself representative of some of the ideals of existentialism. On the whole, *Waiting for Godot* is an artistic medium through which Beckett chose to educate his audience on existentialism as a life philosophy.

One of the basic tenets of existential beliefs is the idea of individual experience defining the universe. This is represented in the play as the seeming lack of plot. Some reviewers, upon first seeing Beckett's play, said of the storyline, "Nothing happens; twice." Indeed, a realist would be expected to take this view, being accustomed to the plethora of other "normal" plays. Even Vladimir and Estragon seem distressed by the seeming nothingness in their experience. This, however, was the distinction Beckett wishes to highlight. A great deal does happen in the play; Pozzo's visits, discourse on the Bible, and the memorable rant from Lucky. To a realist, these are all occurring while waiting for something of substance. For an existentialist, there is no substance, just the defining experience of the individual.

This brings up one of the unique traits of existential philosophy. According to old Aristotelian truths, and thus a part of others schools of thought such as realism, essence proceeds existence. Everything has a "pour-soi," a "a reason for being" before an "en-soi," its being in the universe. Existentialism reverses this order. The world has been "en-soi" forever, yet we give it "pour-soi," or meaning. A good example is a pen. A pen does not call itself a pen, it just is. A conscious individual must come along and define it as a pen. As a result of this divide, realists are constantly searching for meaning, the meaning of life, the meaning of their being, the naturally occurring "pour-soi." How is this represented in Beckett's play? The elusive natural meaning, the "raison d' etre," is none other than Godot.

In existential terms, Vladimir and Estragon are realist individuals waiting for Godot, the meaning of existence, to appear before them. Not realizing that there is no inherent meaning in existence, they wait and wait while ironically showing how they have complete power to project "pour-soi" upon the "en-soi" of their environment. One example of this is forcing Lucky to assume different roles at the drop of a hat, whether he is to be a dancer, a thinker, or just a menial lackey. Lucky is demeaned to the point of being an object rather than a conscious being, thus making him an "en-soi" nothingness and a placeholder for Vladimir's, Estragon's, or Pozzo's "pour-soi" whims. Eventually, the two tramps find themselves overwhelmed with anxiety in the face of their fruitless patience. This situation represents yet another existentialist concept: that angst is the most basic of human emotions, and that it becomes a mode of coping for any individual forced to see existence's lack of meaning.

Finally, there is the mysterious ending: the tramps simultaneously decide to leave and do just the opposite. This shows not only the individual's defining experience but also the individual's time. History and past have absolutely no influence on what matters now, as long as the individual decides this. Vladimir and Estragon sadly, in the face of no true meaning, choose to latch onto their dream of Godot despite the past proving this goal impossible to achieve.

Waiting for Godot is a shocking reversal of the beliefs mankind has learned to depend upon for meaning. It is clear that Beckett must have hoped his audience would be better than his poor protagonists. By introducing existentialism to the masses, Beckett gave us all a chance to be free from the long, long wait for Godot.

The next student wrote about T. S. Eliot's poem *The Waste Land* in a traditional structure, but his creativity is clearly demonstrated throughout the essay. What is of particular note is that this student first wrote a poem to express his analysis of Eliot's highly complex poem. Justin's* poem informed his analytical essay that was written later in the year during our test preparation for the AP examination.

Justin

A Method to the Madness

Imagine a poem that is so chaotic and complex that many poetry critics considered it a "tasteless joke" when it first came out (Waste Land Critical Overview 2009). Welcome to *The Waste Land*, a poem by Thomas Sterns Eliot who is better known as T. S. Eliot. Those critics were right in the sense that in *The Waste Land* the content does not always add up; then again, the content is not supposed to make total sense. Many parts to this poem are jumbled, fragmented, and even contradictory. A single line could have multiple valid interpretations, making it even more of a challenge to extrapolate some semblance of meaning. One fact is clear: Eliot's use of symbols creates a chaos that generates meaning or, at least, what can be interpreted to be meaning. The symbol of plant life and the motif of sterility are excellent examples of Eliot's use of disparate parts to create chaos of the whole. In *Modern Poetry and Tradition*, it is written that in *The Waste Land*, "[A] statement of beliefs emerges through confusion and cynicism—not in spite of them." When examining these symbols and voices, it is prudent to keep this quotation in mind.

Flowers are an archetypal symbol for a range of positive ideas, including beauty, rebirth, happiness, and innocence. Eliot takes this stock response to the symbol and completely reverses the symbol's connotation. In *The Waste Land*, the reader is taken aback by this reversal and must reexamine preconceived notions about the nature of the symbol in response to the work. One example of this use occurs in the first two lines of the poem, reading, "April is the cruelest month, breeding lilacs out of the dead land, mixing . . . " (l. 1–2). These lines are allusions to two famous authors and, at the same time, inversions on their works.

The first line about April comes from *The Canterbury Tales* by Geoffrey Chaucer while the second line comes from Walt Whitman's poetry. Whitman originally wrote about lilacs as a symbol of rebirth. These two lines exemplify that the flowers in Eliot's poem are not in accordance with our typical emotional responses in thinking that flowers symbolize rebirth and beauty. Instead, in this poem, the flowers are a symbol of the inability of rebirth to occur.

One interpretation is that April is the cruelest month because it gives false hope for a renewal. The flowers cannot be reborn because they are rooted in dead land. This complete inversion of Whitman's original idea is hardly subtle. In chaos, reality is bizarre, erratic. Events do not unfold the way they are expected to unfold in Eliot's universe as well as our own. This distortion is a hallmark of chaos. Instead of rebirth, the flowers symbolize the inability to be reborn and, in doing so, futility, even hopelessness.

April breeds lilacs, a fleeting hope of beauty in the waste land. Lilacs are supposed to be the symbol of rebirth, but Eliot has transposed its original meaning. This twisting of the fundamental message evokes a profound sense of destabilization. A message comes from this derangement as the quotation from *Modern Poetry and Tradition* mentions. It supports the theme that humanity is trapped in a "perpetual twilight," unable to be reborn and unable to die.

Hyacinths are another flower mentioned in the first section of *The Waste Land*. Eliot writes, "—Yet when we came back, late, from the Hyacinth garden, Your arms were full, and your hair wet, I could not Speak, and my eyes failed, I was neither Living nor dead, and I knew nothing . . . " (l. 37–40). It is clear that the speaker in this section of the poem is not content. The speaker and a girl are in a hyacinth garden and, traditionally speaking, flowers are associated with rebirth and other positive feelings. Examining this very superficially, why would the speaker be upset? One possibility is that this scene was so beautiful to the speaker that he or she could not stand the fact that human civilization was so marred as to be unable to be repaired and exhibit beauty. Hyacinths are used here as a symbol of melancholy. Taking this from another perspective, the speaker could not see the rebirth that the hyacinths offered because his eyes failed. Again, this inability to be reborn presents itself. The chaos that the symbol creates helps establish the theme that, in its current state, humanity simply cannot be reborn.

Flowers are a very cut and dry example of how Eliot inverts our stock responses to achieve a sense of chaos. Trees are another plant that Eliot uses as a symbol to similar effect. In the first section of the poem, Eliot introduces the Fisher King as our guide through the waste land. Presumably, the Fisher King says, "What are the roots that clutch, what branches grow out of this stony rubbish?" (l. 20–21). The Fisher King serves as another of Eliot's symbols and is used, in part, because of the complexity he, she or it represents. The Fisher King's statement about the "roots that clutch" is a reference to trees. Roots are not supposed to "clutch." The diction here is very important in establishing how Eliot manipulates our stock response to trees and growth. "Clutch" has a negative connotation that sometimes means to hold something tightly without letting go. In this example, a compelling case can be made that this clutching is causing a natural decay or death. In other words, this tree is no longer a symbol of growth and rebirth as it is archetypally considered, but a symbol much like the Sibyl in the beginning of the poem. Humanity is trapped in the waste land and cannot be reborn.

A final example of plant life's archetypal meaning being inverted is found in the second section of the poem. The Fisher King says, "And other withered stumps of time . . . " (l. 104). It is interesting to note that trees grow with time. As time progresses, trees should bloom brilliantly and beautifully. Instead, as time progresses in Eliot's psychic landscape, there is a withered stump. Trees, in this case, symbolize man's own descent into decadence. Normally humankind would be portrayed as a tree that is ever growing. However, in this poem, humankind is portrayed as anything but. Herein lies the method to the chaos. Everything appears backwards; humanity seems to move backwards. The symbols mirror the theme that humanity is trapped in its own waste land.

Not only is life empty in Eliot's poem, but there are so many "broken" images. This idea of imagery being broken is so well developed in this poem that examples could stretch on for pages. Sterility is a form of something being broken that is profoundly developed in *The Waste Land*. Sterility, or the idea of nothing being able to truly grow out of Eliot's waste land, is deeply embedded in the poem. Every example of how Eliot inverts our stock responses with plants is an example of sterility, at least on the metaphoric level. How can lilacs grow out of dead land if the land is dead? Besides being ironic, this line shows that the land in the waste land is sterile. No life can grow from it. This landscape is not only physical, as in the human body, but spiritual, psychic, and environmental.

Some of the most important broken images are found in relation to cities. The Fisher King states, "Falling towers Jerusalem Athens Alexandria Vienna London Unreal . . . " (l. 373–76). Later, the speaker adds, "London Bridge is falling down falling down falling down" (l. 426). These lines indicate something wrong in some of the greatest cities in the world. In the first quotation, Eliot most likely intentionally left it up for interpretation whether the cities are being described as falling towers or there are falling towers in each of the cities. There is support for both viewpoints, but either way this section of the poem is about the fall of cities whether by war or human decadence. The cities are not healthy establishments; Eliot hints that they are fundamentally flawed. The imagery that Eliot provides of falling towers is one in which reality has been distorted: "unreal." Cities, symbols of human ingenuity, have become symbols of decadence and are quite literally falling apart.

Falling towers mirrors Eliot's motif of descent. The other quotation just as well demonstrates descent. "London Bridge falling down" is an allusion to a famous children's song, making the reference even more telling. Essentially this image of a falling bridge mirrors mankind's own fall. Falling appears chaotic. Eliot creates an air of chaos through this radical symbol. It is chaotic imagery and one that clearly brings home Eliot's message that civilization is on a steep and dangerous decline.

Sexual sterility as evoked by Eliot's use of motifs helps establish the theme. Throughout the poem, there are numerous sexual encounters, each ending poorly. One example is found when the poet's persona is with the hyacinth girl in the garden of hyacinths. There seems to be intimacy in this scene, and yet the poet soon freezes up. The poem reads, "Your arms full and your hair wet, I could not Speak, and my eyes failed / I was neither Living nor dead . . . " (l. 38–40). Unlike some of the other relations in *The Waste Land,* this one at least appears to be honest in the sense that the participants have what might genuinely be considered love. For whatever reason, the waste land of the poem corrupts their relationship. This shows that not even pure love can survive the all consuming waste land. Chaos is like a tornado, sucking everything in, good or bad. Through Eliot's intended chaos, the theme that in true disorder nothing beautiful can survive is painfully apparent.

The impotence of sexual acts is also present in later sections of the poem. One sexual encounter in the third section reads, "Flushed and decided, he assaults at once; exploring hands encounter no defense: His vanity requires no response, And makes a welcome indifference" (l. 239–42). This scene shows sex, something supposed to be emotional, turned into a hedonistic ritual devoid of emotion. Sex, typically a symbol of passion or emotion, here is a symbol of the opposite. Eliot is twisting our stock responses to illicit disorientation. The reader is likely to be shocked by this use of sex as a symbol of apathy and must reconsider Eliot's message.

What can we take away from all the chaos? In *Modern Poetry and Tradition,* it is written that in *The Waste Land,* "[A] statement of beliefs emerges through confusion and cynicism—not in spite of them." This is the method to Eliot's madness. Many of the symbols and motifs which include flowers, trees, cities, and sexual encounters all symbolize exactly the opposite of what we have come to regard them as symbolizing. This is chaotic and shows how truly ruined the waste land is. In *The Waste Land,* it is a challenge to find one single image that is not ruined or tainted. Eliot's theme that civilization was in decline is portrayed in a way that is more accurate than a less dense poem would be. Eliot wanted his readers to think about how human civilization is in shambles. He accomplishes this though his inversion of our stock responses and, at times, his radical symbols. The Fisher King states a quotation that mirrors this idea. The quotation is, "You cannot say, or guess, for you know only A heap of broken images . . . " (l. 21–22). *The Waste Land* is easily described as a heap of broken images when it is not read with a discerning eye. It is only when we find meaning in the existence of the broken images, not the images themselves, that we can discover our own "shantih" in terms of scratching the surface in comprehending *The Waste Land.*

Works Cited

Brooks, Cleanth. *Modern Poetry and Tradition.* (Chapel Hill: University of North Carolina Press, 1939).

"The Waste Land Critical Overview." *eNotes—Literature Study Guides.* Accessed November 28, 2009, www.enotes.com/waste-land/critical-overview.

There is much language play in the essay above as well as the one that follows. While both student writers use traditional structures for their arguments, their writing is rich with creativity and contains sophistication of language and concepts.

Dan*

Words—What Are They Good For?

While various literary works in the English language combine a story with one or more thematic ideas in relation to morals, culture, or some other idea, Shakespeare covers these topics in an in-depth yet ambiguous manner in his play *Hamlet,* due to his use of word play in the tragedy. For this particular play, Shakespeare used literary tools such as puns, double entendres, and metaphors, among others, not only to convey the story but also to suggest various interpretations of the text that can be both proven and validated while creating an atmosphere of suspicion between characters that carries the story well beyond the plot. Two closely-related topics that stem from the main character Prince Hamlet are the concepts of uncertainty and inaction. Through the use of various types of word play, particularly puns, Shakespeare uses Hamlet and the events surrounding him to bring forth ideas as to how his lack of concrete decisions and swift actions lead to his downfall, specifically around the topics of morality, religion, and superstition.

Within the story, Hamlet encounters many conflicts that result in him taking the time to consider all of his options and, ultimately, make a decision or prolong his choice of a verdict on his uncle's guilt. The majority of Hamlet's problems originated with his conversation with the Ghost of his father in regards to King Hamlet's untimely demise at the hands of Claudius. While Hamlet could act quickly to avenge his father, his superstition over the Ghost worries him as he says, "My father's spirit—in arms! All is not well. / I doubt some foul play" (Act I, iii, 277–78). This example contains one of Shakespeare's most used puns in the tragedy—the word "play"—along with the word "doubt." While Hamlet is literally using the word "play" in terms of a matter of conduct, it also carries another connotation that relates to the Ghost and his murderer. After Claudius killed his brother, who is now the Ghost appearing to Hamlet, he put on a façade of being sincerely upset even though he proceeded to marry his victim's wife. In this, he was playing a false part; he was pretending to be upset over his brother's death and acting as if he had done nothing wrong. Secondly, the word "doubt" also shows a contribution to Hamlet's indecision. In the context of the sentence, the word is used to say that he is wary of foul play, yet it could also mean that he is unsure as to whether or not there is foul play. The former "play" shows how

Claudius uses a disguised role to avoid his guilt and blame for anything from killing the king to marrying his wife, and "doubt" shows how Hamlet was unsure of what the purpose of the Ghost's visit was: his father seeking revenge, dark spirits seeking to ruin him, or some obscure reason. Hamlet's uncertainty over the validity of the Ghost's statements originated before he met it due to his contemplation of the subject.

Other topics that present Hamlet's issues with indecision and uncertainty are his intertwined religious beliefs and morals. Throughout the play, Hamlet considers performing some act after no deliberation but is quickly held back as he delves further into the situation. The most famous example of his contemplation of a situation comes from his "To be or not to be" soliloquy, where he says at one point, "Whether 'tis nobler in the mind to suffer / The slings and arrows of outrageous fortune, / Or to take arms against a sea of troubles / And, by opposing, end them" (Act III, i, 65–68). This passage in the soliloquy shows Hamlet's indecision over a morbid topic—to kill himself and ease his suffering or to live and fight the problems of his life. Debatably, the only reason that he refrains from suicide is his morality and religious beliefs, as he believes, as a Christian, that suicide would be a direct ticket to hell. Unrelated to suicide, Shakespeare discretely uses a pun in this statement that actually pertains to Hamlet's intention to kill his uncle. The word "arms" literally means, in the context of the sentence, weapons, and it can also refer to human limbs. In the latter context, the second half of the sentence can be interpreted as inflicting damage upon the human source of the problems, specifically Claudius, "and by opposing, end them." A later example in the soliloquy occurs when Hamlet says, "To sleep, perchance to dream. Ay, there's the rub, / For in that sleep of death what dreams may come" (Act III, i, 73–74). In these lines, "death" is interchangeable with "sleep," as mentioned in the second half, and "dreams" has two meanings. The first, and most obvious, considering the background of the soliloquy, is that it can be replaced with "afterlife," meaning Hamlet is considering what afterlife is truly there after death. Secondly, "dreams" can refer to Hamlet's worldly dreams, such as becoming the King of Denmark. With these two examples, Shakespeare shows how Hamlet's uncertainty comes into play as he ponders aspects of his life but never comes to a concrete decision. It also shows irony in the fact that Hamlet refuses to kill himself not only because he is a Christian but because he is wary of the existence of an afterlife, which is a basic Christian belief, and he had already seen the Ghost of his father, proving that there must be an afterlife of some manner.

Other examples of Hamlet's morals and religious beliefs leading to his indecision and uncertainty continue in the play, especially with his decision not to kill Claudius while his uncle was vulnerably praying. After hearing Claudius confess, after being overridden with guilt during the play, Hamlet says, "Now might I do it pat, now he is a-praying, / And now I'll do't. And so he goes to heaven, / And so am I revenged. That would be scanned" (Act III, iii, 77–80). Here, Hamlet finally shows confidence in a decision but is quickly overrun by uncertainty over the potential results of his revenge, even though he begins to contradict himself again. Later in the passage he says, "He took my father grossly, full of bread, / With all his crimes broad blown" (Act III, iii, 85–86). In these lines, Shakespeare uses several puns that can be effectively interpreted in various ways. The first is evidenced with the statement "grossly, full of bread"—the literal use is that King Hamlet was slain while still physically part of the world, but its more relevant meaning is that he was killed while idle or lazy. In accordance with this context, "grossly" can also be read as "disgusting," He is considering this act of Claudius killing King Hamlet to gain control of the kingdom and his wife was a vile act. The second half, "with all his crimes broad blown," addresses King Hamlet's murder without the Christian ritual of Last Rites or another form of repentance. He was murdered with his unforgiven sins still on his conscience and, according to the Christian religion; he would go to hell if they were significant enough. Hamlet's morals and a solid decision were overridden temporarily, but his religious beliefs and uncertainty ultimately kept him from murdering Claudius when his uncle was most vulnerable and when Hamlet may have gotten away with it.

Although Hamlet's lack of concrete decisions and swift, uninterrupted actions ultimately brought him to his downfall, the rash decisions of other characters, particularly Claudius, Laertes, and Polonius, led to their own demise and reinforced Shakespeare's point that, at the end of it all, even if we take the brief, extreme path, we ultimately end up in the same position as those who deliberated on decisions. His puns helped to reinforce this idea by pointing out the multiple ways that Hamlet's methodical thinking resulted in him being dragged into a plot against him. Shakespeare's language ambiguities allow for the readers to easily develop their own opinions and ideas based upon interpretation.

SUMMARY NOTES

The preceding section of student writing may be highly interesting to educators as it represents excellent student writing in the most recognizable structure, but each essay shows evidence of rich creativity and student ownership of the writing. The grammar and mechanics also attest to the fact that the students spent considerable time crafting and editing their works. These essays were not edited by the teacher.

The essays were written later during a semester, after students had been given opportunities to explore creative choice and creative techniques. The students found that they were able to employ the techniques to emphasize and strengthen their arguments while still using the more traditional structure of the formal essay. As one student said to me, "It's not like we forget what a paragraph looks like."

Many students later wrote about the fact that the instruction in creative techniques and creative choice empowered them, and the instruction was instrumental in leading them to self-identify as writers.

12

Changing the Landscape of Academic Writing Assignments and the Classroom Environment

One of the most astute, albeit painful, comments made by a college professor was that too often teachers *assign* writing rather than *teach* it. Although most teachers' first response is likely to be defensive, if we examine our practices, we are likely to discover that we make assumptions about what students are capable of doing and quickly enter into testing and assessment mode rather than teaching skills in how to write well.

Of course, we offer models and provide instruction, but the time constraints of completing the requirements within curricula and meeting all local and state testing mandates appear to leave insufficient time for teaching true writing process.

Most English teachers provide opportunities for summative and formative assessments in grading a rough draft and a final draft of a student paper, but teacher and/or peer feedback on drafts is often insufficient for really teaching and learning how to write well. Unfortunately, much of this practice feels repetitive to students who are not learning from repeating the same problems in their writing.

A student stated that he did not see the point of all of those years of education. He said that he had learned to read and write in second grade. For a moment, we can feel his frustration with a world that had changed while he was creating his sentences that expressed the complexity of the mind of an elementary school student while he was in high school.

When we read his work aloud, however, he winced. It was very difficult for him to recognize that the structures and vocabulary he had once used to consider himself an accomplished writer were no longer working to express the increasing complexity of his thoughts.

The first step is to make sure that we build time into our instructional practice that includes writing conferences. While many teachers may be concerned about how to fit these conferences into the curriculum, it is possible to meet one-on-one with students when the other students are engaged in a group discussion, project work, or writing or reading tasks.

Students are far more receptive to critical comments in the form of a conversation than those comments jotted down in the form of teacher's notes on a paper. When our students are allowed to elaborate as much on what they do well as on what they need help with, they are more likely to be open to changing their writing practices.

So what does this new, writer-friendly landscape look like? It may take the form of writing and editing conversations between students or between student and teacher, in addition to direct instruction. This means, ideally, more writing time for students within the classroom. The word "conversation" is used rather than "conference" because of the dual emphasis on the student speaking and the teacher listening.

Allowing our students to talk through their thinking and writing processes may be more valuable to them than having a teacher pointing out grammatical errors or correcting style problems.

Transforming our classrooms into writing communities does not involve many physical changes and is relatively straightforward to implement. The concept basically involves teachers making sure that they allot some time for writing in the classroom and support students taking creative risks with assignments.

What does a supportive environment look like? Here is where teachers get to be creative, too. The look will vary from classroom to classroom, but the students and the teachers should be able to feel the difference. This may be as simple as teacher-to-student one-on-one conversations about writing.

A change in the environment could involve a physical setting, such as moving chairs in a pattern more conducive to conversation and dialogue or allowing students to select their seating and arrangement.

Knowing students' names on the first day allows us to redirect or shape the atmosphere in the room. Seating arrangements may be noted as an earned privilege as long as students stay on task and their conversations are about writing, techniques, or process. Writing time becomes expression, not a dreaded chore.

Peter Elbow suggests emphasizing reader feedback throughout his text,[1] and we know that timely feedback is critical to helping students develop into good writers. Think about our own responses when someone does not get back to us immediately.

It is only human to tend to forget about a project and lose interest if the feedback does not follow very soon after completion. Finding out a teacher's responses to a paper is not particularly helpful if those comments are not delivered until two or three weeks later.

This is one of the more difficult aspects of teaching writing because helpful feedback takes time to consider and construct, and teachers are responsible for evaluating a multitude of student papers. However, our students would be better served if we asked them to write fewer papers and we provided a quicker response to them.

Here are a few proven ideas for making our classrooms writer friendly:

- Working collaboratively with classmates and other teachers
- Writing with your students even if it is not for the same assignment
- Sharing your writing "failures" with the class as well as your successes
- Allowing students to have freedom in the decision-making processes at each stage of the lesson and in producing the product
- Encouraging journaling—good habits and storing gems; the key to effective journaling is to allow students complete freedom to write about whatever they wish in their journals
- Setting clear expectations for students and articulating the lesson's goals
- Structuring student-and-teacher writer's conferences/conversations on a regular basis
- Building into the lesson time for writing process and multiple drafts

Not everyone is comfortable breaking the dam that holds back a student's creative river because we—students and teacher alike—all know how much work it will be to undertake this process, but educators need to give up some control if our students are to become better writers, deeper thinkers, and scholars.

According to Bartholomae, "We rely on our freedom to go back and hold our writing at arm's length. And, while students need to learn how and when to worry about correctness, they also need to learn how and when to tap into the generative power of language, which requires that the editor be shut off and we be free to experiment and take risks."[2]

We need to allow them the space and support to make mistakes in their writing and learn from that process. We do not need to grade every aspect of a piece of writing on each and every assignment.

What does it take on the teacher's part to foster creativity in academic writing?

- Willingness to look at academic writing assignments in a different way

- Work in developing rubrics that will specifically measure the goal of the lesson and not the risk taking in format or structure
- Opportunities for writing conferences/conversations and writing process
- Sufficient number of excellent models of writing in which creative techniques are incorporated to good effect
- Encouragement and support of students who take risks in their development as writers
- Additional time in class and time in lesson preparation
- A safe, nonthreatening classroom to develop ideas and writing techniques and skills

In this age of emphasis on assessment for measurement, that list is asking a lot of dedicated professionals who put a tremendous amount of time into their work, but every one of us would agree that we are willing to do what it takes to help our students become deeper thinkers and better writers across the curricula.

It is the teacher's and the writer's work to disturb the reader, agitate him or her into critical thinking, nudge complacency out of the room, and intrude on a lazy day with rhetoric revealed when the reader is awakened. We want our students to find their voices, dig deeply, and take the time to turn ideas and words over and over in the mind until the eye apprehends.

Writing well is one of the most powerful lifelong skills with which we can arm our students. As writer and artist Danny Gregory states, "Journaling has transformed my life and given me the clearest form of identity I've ever had."[3] We know that expression and identity are inextricably linked, and we owe it to our students to empower them, to help them find that expression and their writing identities.

How do we build all of this one-on-one conversation time into a curriculum that is already packed? We need to ask ourselves, is that packed curriculum leading to all of the desired results?

A starting point for finding more time for writing in the classroom is examining what is most essential. Once that essential instruction is identified, then we can begin deciding where duplication takes place and what can be set aside for another day or indefinitely.

A common complaint of students is that they spend time going over material that they already know. This happens because teachers are concerned about some students who may not yet have an understanding of that material. Differentiating instruction sounds great, but it is difficult to accomplish such individualized instruction on a daily basis. Offering writing workshops in the classroom, however, provides the structure for this type of instruction.

There are strategies for making it work for everyone. To facilitate student-teacher conversations about writing, we can structure our time during other group activities, project work, or Socratic Circles. With the other students actively engaged and talking, a single student will be more likely to open up about his or her problems with writing, and the conversation does not have to be about problems in the writing.

We can ask a simple question to get our students to reflect on their writing processes: which sentence do you think is your best and why? This question frequently leads into discussions that turn into direction instruction relating to the use of subordination to begin sentences, clarification of punctuation rules, use of various techniques, and parts of speech. But the question also takes the conversation in unexpected directions and provides opportunities for students to self-reflect without penalty or fear of condescension.

What other practices can we examine in order to help students improve their writing? Before any instruction takes place, we need to build the essential questions into the framework of the lesson and make those questions known both orally and in writing, and then build creative flexibility into the lesson plan.

How the goal is met may be determined by the students to a great degree. Students are more engaged when they become collaborators in teaching rather than the recipients of instruction. This is as true of a high school freshman as it is of a college freshman.

A favorite lesson with students is one in which they write a scene or mini-script in which they create characters commenting on the text they have read. In this lesson, they write a script that essentially incorporates their prior knowledge, reflects on what they understand, highlights the "big ideas," and considers various ways of looking at a text. They become writers, collaborators, lesson designers, and critical thinkers in one lesson.

In the beginning, giving up some of our direct instruction may be hard because there is the fear that the students won't arrive at the desired goal as quickly. I can recall, however, that bright but disruptive student lighting up when I told him that he was going to present a ten-minute lesson the next class.

Initially, the proposal might have been presented as a way to alter disruptive behavior. Yet the lesson had unintended and very positive benefits. The parameters I set were that he had to find a way to help everyone discover themes in the literature we were reading.

This student later related that the confidence shown in him (which he believed was unwarranted) gave him the courage to do a good job. The next class, he led a clever ten-minute lesson on thematic discovery by assigning character roles to everyone in the class and asking his peers to speak as a particular character, revealing through their speech what their characters expressed about themes.

Students are eager for more ways in which they have opportunities to teach each other. The ultimate outcome of that gift of confidence, added responsibility, and encouragement to use creativity was not bookmarked until years later, however, when the young man stopped by after school to talk about his first job as a high school English teacher.

He shared stories about some of his difficult students. Would he have found his path from class cutup to teacher/leader without the experience of being challenged to lead? Very likely, but, nevertheless, he credited our creatively structured classroom environment with providing him the opportunity to begin that transition from boy to young teacher.

The classroom landscape needs to move from teacher-controlled to teacher-guided as students assume increasing responsibilities for their education. Initially, this is not any easier for them than it is for us to give up those controls, but it is far more effective in terms of producing the results we are all seeking.

What happens, you might ask, when a student-initiated learning activity fails or does not work as intended? The same thing that happens when a teacher-designed lesson does not produce the intended outcomes; we learn more from our mistakes than our successes.

But there are standardized tests for which students must be prepared! Of course this concern must be addressed, but these creative approaches to learning actually produce higher test scores. If students are more engaged in their education, if they are thinking critically and divergently, it reasonably follows that they will also improve their writing and test scores.

It is possible to meet all of the curriculum requirements and still allow time for multiple drafts, but we have to be willing to restructure assignments, build drafting into every writing assignment, and allow students more choice in how those writing products are structured.

All students' writing products do not need to look like formal essays; the students will remember how an essay is structured when summative testing takes place. Part of the learning process is about making decisions, even when the decisions lead to less than desired results.

We know this as adults, but we have to allow our students the opportunities of working through problems in writing without the high costs of the fumbles. Quite simply, they need a place to practice, an environment in which they can reach higher and not be afraid to fail. Introducing creativity into the classroom is not simply about introducing creative techniques and structures but about introducing creative thinking into designs for learning.

SUMMARY NOTES

Transforming our classrooms into writing communities does not involve many physical changes and is relatively straightforward to implement. The concept basically involves teachers making sure that they allot some time for writing in the classroom and support students taking creative risks with assignments.

13

Making Editing Integral

Write with the door closed, rewrite with the door open.

—Stephen King[1]

King's pithy comment on the difference between writing and editing addresses the distinction in the way we look at the world as well as our processes. We need a closed door or a certain degree of solitude to think and draft a composition of any kind, but when it comes to editing, we have to open those doors, let others inside, hear their voices before we can make the changes that will improve the work.

Another Stephen King quotation on the difficult work of editing emphasizes the fact that the real work, the hard work, begins with editing: "Talent is cheaper than table salt. What separates the talented individual from the successful one is a lot of hard work."[2]

Our students have innate gifts, but to write well takes hard work through the process of rewriting. Typically, students assume that they are not talented writers because their first drafts are weak. They are often unwilling to do the time-consuming work of editing, making the assumption that revision and editing will not change the product sufficiently.

Yet nearly every professional writer has addressed the issue of the importance of editing. Writers know that only one line comes from that netherworld of inspiration as it drops from the ceiling, as Annie Dillard suggested and attributed to an anonymous author via Thornton Wilder in *The Writing Life*.[3]

The rest of it is earned through the actions of rolling up your sleeves and getting down to work. Good writers love that process. The trick is to get our students, our children to believe in themselves as writers, own their writing products, and then begin the work of revision and editing.

To get students thinking about editing from day one, we can tack up great writers' quotations about editing around the entire room. In one activity, students get up from their chairs, walk around the room, read the quotations, choose a favorite or one that speaks to them in some way, and then write a short response about why the quotation affected them. They are already thinking about editing before they have written one word.

Educational theorists address editing's inherent paradox of going back in order to move forward in discussing the recursive aspect of writing. Here is where a piece of writing is transformed if the writer is willing to work at the process. Typically, however, students spend very little time editing even when it is built into assignments. They may, in fact, be more averse to editing at the college level than in high school.

Asked why they don't edit, most students riff on the theme of non-ownership. Look, they say, they completed the writing as an assignment for a grade. It is the grade that becomes more important than the learning.

Unfortunately, the students sometimes do not feel the writing is important to them, and if it is not deemed important, they are not going to spend the time on it. The secret to getting our students to edit their work at all is to get them to want to take ownership of it.

One colleague challenged her students to create scripts and film documentaries for a project in an Honors 11 English class. The students were so excited about these projects that one student later commented to her that she had spent twenty-two hours editing the script and documentary film. You read that correctly—twenty-two hours editing!

This teacher said, "When was the last time a student told us that he or she had spent twenty-two hours editing anything?" Students will edit their work if they feel that sense of ownership and the pride that follows it.

A student wrote in a letter following a class that she found she spent more time with the text, more time analyzing because of the challenge presented by writing creatively. She later added to that written comment a verbal one in which she said that she remembered the text because of the creativity of the design. Quite simply, she stated that she was more engaged.

If a student is spending more time with both the text and the writing, editing becomes a natural outgrowth of both the level of engagement and the critical thinking.

Admittedly, editing is a difficult aspect of the writing process because it involves a completely different skill, even a different point of view. David Bartholomae writes, "Students need to learn how to distance themselves from and analyze the writing on the page in order to determine what information that writing holds about their performance as a writer."[4]

Editing may be the most "hated" aspect of writing, as identified by one of my students. However, every educator knows how important this task is, so how do we go about helping our students to take that crucial step? If a student is invested in his or her work, that student will be willing to edit the composition.

AN ACTIVITY DESIGNED TO ENCOURAGE EDITING: THE SCAVENGER HUNT

Writing an introduction or opening with a hook for the reader is one of the most difficult aspects of writing either fiction or nonfiction. Fiction writers seem to have developed more tools for the job, however, as readers are likely to put a fiction book down if the opening does not interest them in some way. Using fiction techniques to introduce academic nonfiction writing can be highly effective as well.

To help students discover some of the varied ways professional writers hook the reader, you might use a scavenger hunt activity with students in your classes. This activity can be tailored to meet any grade-level or college-appropriate task.

Scavenger Hunt Activity Task Sheet

Your Task:

- Find ten great opening lines from literature (or nonfiction text). The lines you select should be memorable to you.
- Copy the lines in your journal.
- Write the title of the book and the name of the author under each quotation.
- Identify the reason each line is memorable to you under the citation.
- Discuss your selections and reasons for inclusion in class.

Note: Possible reasons and techniques that make the lines memorable:

1. Irony for emphasis
2. Deliberate contradiction
3. Startling fact or statement
4. Rhythm and other sound effects such as alliteration or onomatopoeia
5. Other poetic techniques, such as metaphor, simile, personification, hyperbole, chiasmus, metonymy, synecdoche, among many others
6. Author's syntax (word order)
7. Author's unusual diction
8. Unusual sentence variety or structure
9. *In medias res* (starting in the middle)
10. Anachrony (structure that moves nonchronologically)

SUMMARY NOTES

Editing takes a time commitment on the part of students who are often reluctant to do this work. However, the engaged student, the student who is deeply invested in his or her work, will make this commitment, and the results will demonstrate the improvement in grammar and mechanics.

14

Inviting the Common Core State Standards into the Classroom and Recognizing That They Are First Cousins to Creativity

Teachers are well aware of the increasingly high stakes of standardized testing, and, as a result, we often focus on getting our students through the test rather than guiding them through critical thinking and independent written analysis. The best learning and good writing take trial and error, failed experiments that lead to eventual successes.

What we end up with when we prescribe and proscribe the writing formulas for students is too often writing that is not only dull and uninspired but does not meet state and federal standards. We may recognize the problem, but the solution is less readily available. Just like our students and children, we have to be willing to take risks. Helping them to become articulate, engaging writers, however, is definitely worth the effort and the calculated risk.

Risk taking in a highly charged political climate in which public education in particular has come under increased scrutiny and criticism is asking a great deal of professional educators. Yet there is another way to look at the increased demands for high-stakes testing—as a challenge.

Educators seldom back away from a challenge, whether it is related to new trends, new personnel, student apathy, or politicians campaigning on platforms they believe will get them elected. We can also use the tests to show what does work and ask the state to consider the effectiveness of their mandates as well.

The new College and Career Readiness Standards from the Common Core have arrived, and whether we find them a unifying arbiter, an obnoxious cousin, or something else entirely, we are obliged to bring them into the classroom, make the best use of them to improve student performance, and engage in a useful, pedagogical dialogue.

The good news is that introducing creative choice and creative techniques into writing process instruction aligns perfectly with the Common Core State Standards as well as with Bloom's higher order in the taxonomy and the 21st Century Skills Framework.

Application of creative approaches—as shown in this text—is designed to boost writing test scores as well as produce better written student products and foster critical thinking. In addition, the application of creative techniques helps students both read and write with greater depth and sophistication.

Examining the Common Core State Standards for English Language Arts for Reading and Writing, we see a number of direct correspondences to creativity—for example, creative approaches and "innovative perspectives," "trying a new approach," and "demonstrating independence, and understanding of figurative language," among other key phrases found in the Common Core State Standards.

For purposes of comparison, language from the Common Core is pulled and highlighted here to show the way in which the tasks addressed a particular aspect of the Standards.

ANCHOR STANDARDS

From the Anchor Standards for Reading, we find language that addresses creative techniques under Craft and Structure—4: "Interpret words and phrases as they are used in a text, including determining technical, connotative, and figurative meanings." Students who routinely use creative techniques in their writing have fewer problems determining connotative and figurative meanings in texts.

In the Anchor Standards for Writing, we note the connection to the experiments in narratives (as shown in chapter 3 of this text)—3. "Write narratives to develop real or imagined experiences or events using effective techniques."

COMMON CORE STATE STANDARDS FOR ENGLISH LANGUAGE ARTS (ELA)

Because reading and writing learning experiences are so closely enmeshed, I include the relevant reading standards here. Of particular note is the language that addresses "innovative perspectives," promoting divergent and metaphorical thinking.

Common Core: Reading: Responding to Literature
Interpret, analyze, and evaluate narratives, poetry, and drama aesthetically and philosophically by making connections to other texts, ideas, cultural perspectives, eras, personal events, and situations.
a. Self-select text to respond and develop innovative perspectives.

The creative approaches outlined in this text directly address the development of students' innovative perspectives, opening the doors for students to navigate those waters and discover original ways of examining a text rather than be provided the lens through which the reader and writer must analyze content, an approach found in more traditional teaching methods of responding to literature.

The concept of "self-selecting," in particular, has been shown throughout my book to develop students' critical thinking skills, allowing them to practice those skills with written applications. An example of an assignment directly related to self-selecting is shown in the models provided in chapter 3, in which students must self-select a creative framework for their arguments as well as create the argument itself.

Instructors who offer a task that asks students to respond to a prompt and then develop the argument using appropriate, selected passages of the text to make their arguments align perfectly with this section of the Common Core.

The very nature of encouraging students' creative choice and application of creative techniques in writing is causal in the development of innovative perspectives and divergent thinking.

Although every example provided in this text demonstrates these concepts, readers may go back to the innovative perspective, original narrative, and character extension of Faulkner's Caddy, as originally experienced in his novel *The Sound and the Fury*. By selecting evidence from Faulkner's novel, Julia was able to make inferences and further characterize Caddy Compson, and in the process, she created a wholly new way of looking at the character Faulkner himself said was one of his most memorable.

After Julia completed her narrative essay on the consequences of Caddy's actions, she stated that Caddy, too, was one of her favorite characters in literature because the experience of Faulkner's character for Julia was both literary exploration and a personal connection. She said this as if she had created Caddy Compson—along with Faulkner—out of her own art because, to a degree, she had. In this instance, Julia's narrative essay allowed her to deeply explore Faulkner's character even beyond the boundaries of the page.

Creative approaches to responding to literature are the antecedent to student's immersion in the text. By the very nature of the act of having to consider what choices they have and what approaches they will take, students must read and reread passages in order to make those determinations as well as think more deeply about the author's ideas.

Students sometimes initially complain about trying a creative approach because, as they say, "it takes so much more time!" In other words, they cannot simply provide stock responses. There is no ready-fit formula to regurgitate in the process of creative choice and writing creatively.

Another section of the Common Core asks educators to guide students through the processes in which they

> b. Establish and use criteria to classify, select, and evaluate texts to make informed judgments about the quality of the pieces.

In order to select and classify portions of texts to use in their creatively written work, students must spend additional time considering how the evidence works with their approach. One student stated that she had to spend "three times longer on the creatively written response" because she had to think about how to use the information in a way that worked with her chosen design. "I had to keep going back over the novel to find passages that I could use," she added.

This additional time with texts tends to elevate the "quality of the pieces" they write, as well as raises the level of their understanding of the texts they have read. This young woman admitted that she typically hurried through writing assignments and seemed content with a grade lower than she was capable of getting. When she got excited about her work, however, she stopped between classes to discuss her writing with teachers and peers.

In other words, she went from a passive learner to an active one. Once the creative approach has been selected, the student feels compelled go back over the texts and make determinations about how a passage may be used to support the approach chosen.

> Common Core Writing Standard:
> W. 11-12.2: Use techniques such as metaphor, simile, and analogy to manage the complexity of the topic.

Clearly, the instruction teachers provide in creative techniques and the writing practice students engage in have direct connections to the Core Writing Standards. The grades 11–12 Standard is used here, but the language is very similar at all of the high school levels.

Students will discuss their lack of understanding of figurative language as a form of protest. They initially start by stating that they hate poetry "because no one knows what it's about." Teaching creative writing techniques as part of the writing instruction, however, provides the students with tools for writing and reading as well as interpretation of nonliteral texts. The interrelatedness of writing instruction and reading comprehension cannot be stated strongly enough.

Upon entering a high school or college classroom, nearly all students are able to recite the words "a metaphor is a comparison between two unlike things," but when it comes to recognizing and deciphering metaphoric language in texts, they become novices again. Teaching students how to create metaphors and write metaphoric passages allows them to read at a higher level, as creators of text.

They suddenly understand metaphor in a way that dictionary-definition recitations do not offer. Teachers may begin with simple metaphor exercises like some of the models shown in chapter 4 and then increase the level of sophistication and complexity, depending upon the age and metaphoric experience of the student.

While metaphors offer entrance to poetry and poetic prose, they are also a means to seeing the world in a new way. This comes as a revelation to many students who find original voice through the use of metaphors.

Although other techniques such as simile, hyperbole, and personification also aid in helping students understand texts and improve writing, a great starting point in the introduction of creative technique instruction in writing is the metaphor. Instruction in metaphors seems to have the most lasting and powerful effect upon student writing because it so directly alters our way of thinking about the world.

Perhaps what is most surprising is how accessible metaphors are to all students. I have had students who were mainstreamed into a regular education classroom for the first time in their careers be able to compose metaphors effectively. One of the short poems found in chapter 3 features the work of such a student.

Specific assignments involving narrative as shown in chapter 4 have a direct connection to the Common Core Writing Standard 13:

> W. 11-12.13: Write narratives to develop real and imagined experiences or events using effective techniques, well-chosen details, and well-structured event sequences.

The Writing Standards also address editing, and we can see that student ownership of their writing products results in self-directed efforts to edit, plan, and revise.

> Language from the Common Core:
> Develop and strengthen writing as needed by planning, revising, editing, rewriting, or trying a new approach, focusing on addressing what is most significant for a specific purpose and audience. Editing for conventions should demonstrate command of Language standards.

Too often when students write about any academic subject, they try to simply rephrase the task and constrain the response to answers that have been repeated. They have neither thought deeply about the topic nor have they considered other approaches, limiting not only their writing but their reading and thinking.

Creative approaches to teaching and writing generate "new approaches" and motivate students to concentrate on meaning and engage in divergent thinking. This concept of self-selection ties in neatly with the Common Core emphasis in writing standards as outlined above and below:

> Develop and strengthen writing as needed by planning, revising, editing, rewriting, or trying a new approach. . . . Editing for conventions should demonstrate command of Language standards.

Chapter 13 of this text elaborates on both the importance of editing and how the creative approach fosters students' editing and revision of their papers.

One comment nearly every student mentioned in the research surveys ended with the caveat that they "didn't spend much time editing" before they began to embark upon creative journeys into writing. Most professional writers will attest to the fact that the editing/revision process is where the work moves from the ordinary to the extraordinary, yet nearly all admit that editing is the least fun aspect of writing. Because it is difficult and not particularly enjoyable, editing takes additional motivators.

Every teacher has tricks and strategies to encourage students to edit and revise, but the most effective means of involving our students in the editing process is to get them to take ownership of their work. Using these creative approaches to writing, by the nature of the processes, students see the writing as their own and are more invested in the final products. As a result, they are simply more willing to do the work of editing.

Readers may want to reexamine the essay model of the dialogue between the Dillard horse and the Thoreau horse presented in chapter 7 as an example of a student product that was thoroughly edited. Why this is significant is due to the fact that this same student was one of the most reluctant of editors.

When he was given models and encouragement to make his arguments through more creative approaches, he began to take the initiative to edit his own work. It was no longer a question of the teacher pointing out errors, but the student taking on the responsibility to make his own writing better.

The following passages are taken from the Common Core Language Standards:

Conventions of Standard English

1. Demonstrate command of the conventions of standard English grammar and usage when writing or speaking.
   a. Apply the understanding that usage is a matter of convention, can change over time, and is sometimes contested.
   b. Resolve issues of complex or contested usage, consulting references (e.g., *Merriam-Webster's Dictionary of English Usage, Garner's Modern American Usage*) as needed.
2. Demonstrate command of the conventions of Standard English capitalization, punctuation, and spelling when writing.
   a. Observe hyphenation conventions.
   b. Spell correctly.

One of the surprising correlations I discovered in action research was the direct line between level of student interest and engagement to the amount of time spent editing and revising for grammar and mechanics, as noted earlier in this chapter.

In the research phase of this text, students were asked why they chose not to edit when they understood the fact that there were errors in grammar and mechanics in their final written products. There answers were somewhat surprising.

Many "good" academic students simply skipped the editing and revising stage even when they were aware that their writing contained errors. They simply were not invested in the product, they stated. They considered the errors "unimportant."

When students do not understand a grammatical rule, then direct instruction in that principle of grammar is needed, but when the problem lies with student effort and initiative, or lack thereof, we need another approach to writing instruction, and creative approaches to writing instruction have proven to be highly effective in motivating students to revise, edit, and rework their products.

We must ask ourselves, how many years of instruction in the application of commas do high school and college instructors provide, and why does that instruction appear to be so inconsequential, even completely absent? College comp instructors might theorize that high school teachers do not teach comma rules, but that is simply not the case.

If the instruction is being provided, why are the students not incorporating the rules into their writing? What some teachers do not do to the extent necessary, however, is help students understand why rules of grammar and mechanics are so integral to the power or lack of power of their written products. Students need to experience that for themselves in order to buy into the idea that editing is critical to good written communication.

When a student takes a creative risk in writing, he or she is more eager to be understood. Students tend to seek out instruction in grammar when they are highly invested in their written products, as noted previously.

Setting up grammar workshops during the writing process enables educators to offer one-on-one instruction, as well as group instruction, in particular principles of grammar and/or mechanics. During these workshops, students are also encouraged to self-edit, peer edit, and read one another's products.

The Common Core asks instructors to help students in the Knowledge of Language:

> Apply knowledge of language to understand how language functions in different contexts, to make effective choices for meaning or style, and to comprehend more fully when reading or listening.
>
> Vary syntax for effect, consulting references (e.g., Tufte's *Artful Sentences*) for guidance as needed; apply an understanding of syntax to the study of complex texts when reading.

As may be seen in the students' works found in chapter 7, an understanding of how language functions is more likely to be arrived at when the student must make many choices in style, format, and creative techniques.

The Common Core asks students to

> Demonstrate independence in gathering vocabulary knowledge when considering a word or phrase important to comprehension or expression.

Students must demonstrate independence in much more than vocabulary knowledge in selecting the words, structure, and creative approaches to the writing assignments as presented in this text. In addition, the creative approaches outlined here align perfectly with critical thinking in the areas of analysis, creating, self-direction, and application.

The Common Core State Standards for Writing also address the range of student writing:

> W. 11-12.10: Write routinely over extended time frames for a range of tasks and purposes.

The writing experiences you guide your students through should be varied and, as stated in the Core Standards documents, routine. We should aim to provide writing experiences for our students on a daily basis. By the end of the semester or year, our students will have engaged in writing pieces of varying lengths and for various purposes, and they will have been writing and taking ownership of those products.

SUMMARY NOTES

Teaching creative choice and creative techniques meets Common Core State Standards in multiple ways.

15

Lesson Planning Involving Creative Choice and Techniques

SECTION 1: BUILDING CREATIVE TECHNIQUES INTO THE WRITING LESSON

The lesson plan particulars will vary widely with the grade, subject, and level of your students. To implement this strategy effectively, teachers need to be very clear in communicating the essential and guiding questions to students and then allow them to take risks in writing without penalizing the risk taking in the initial assessments.

In other words, if the goal is analyzing character in a story, create a rubric which assesses that goal and not the product's framework. If the goal is to compare and contrast texts, make sure that the rubric assesses that goal and not the writing risk taking in the process or framework of the writing.

Once you have established the essential questions and shared your rubric, you and your students will know exactly what it is that will be graded. Next, show your students great models of creative adventures in writing and encourage your students to try a creative structure or creative technique.

If they have opportunities to practice these techniques on shorter writing assignments, students will be more willing to experiment with them on the major writing projects. They won't forget how to structure an essay or composition for a test because they have tried creative approaches.

SAMPLE LESSON FOR IMPROVING WRITING THROUGH THE USE OF CREATIVE CHOICE AND CREATIVE TECHNIQUES IN STUDENT WRITING

The creative approach you encourage your students/children to take to writing assignments meets the Common Core State Standards in which students are asked to "write narratives in which they engage the reader by establishing the significance of a problem, situation, or observation."

The Core Standards also ask that teachers help students to "develop narrative elements—setting, stance event sequence, complex characters—with purposefully selected details that call readers' attention to what is most distinctive or worth noticing" using a "wide variety of techniques to build toward a particular impact."

Sample Task: Analyzing Narrative and Narrative Techniques in Joseph Conrad's *Heart of Darkness*

For this lesson, you want your students to perform complex and critical thinking about narrative, and in the process, analyze the reliability of the point of view and how a character's voice reveals theme and truthfulness or verisimilitude through point of view.

Essential Questions:

1. Is the narrator reliable?
2. What aspects of narrative and what narrative techniques cause the reader to either believe or doubt the verisimilitude of the narrator?
3. What does the reliability of the narrative reveal about character and themes?

Guiding Questions:

- How does the framed narrative cast doubt on the reliability of the narrator?
- How does Kurtz's story become both Marlow's and the Unnamed Narrator's stories?
- Because Marlow narrates most of the novella, do we identify with him more than any other character? Why or why not?
- How does point of view affect the reader? Cause sympathetic relationships?
- Does Marlow's narrative exhibit verisimilitude? Why or why not?
- What thematic ideas are revealed through Marlow's narrative?
- What thematic ideas are revealed through the voice of the Unnamed Narrator?
- What thematic ideas seem to lie outside either the narrative of Marlow or the Unnamed Narrator on the ship?
- What other narrator seems to be at work here? Do we identify the author's presence? How?

ELA Standards:

State and federal standards met with this lesson would be identified here.

Context:

Students have just completed the reading of Conrad's novella and will have an understanding of the historical and social contexts of Conrad's life and literature from previous classes. Students will be familiar with framing as a narrative technique from previous classes. Students have also recently completed a unit on poetic techniques and poetry. We will have previously discussed using creative writing approaches in analysis.

Materials:

Joseph Conrad's novella *Heart of Darkness*
Task sheet with the essential questions and the writing prompt
Dictionaries
Creative approach models from previous classes

Time Frame: One class

Anticipatory Set:

As students enter the room, hand each student a marker and a task sheet.

Procedures:

1. Direct students to choose a passage from the novella and to write that passage on the whiteboard, as indicated on their task sheets.
2. Ask students to read each other's choices and identify the narrator(s).
3. Direct students to work in small groups to discuss the verisimilitude of each narrative voice from the various passages on the board.
4. In whole-class discussion, guide students in arriving at thematic ideas from the various narrative passages the students have chosen and analyzed in groups.
5. Direct students to their writing task, which may be completed in class or as homework.

The Task:

In approximately three to four pages, analyze the reliability of a narrative voice or voices in Conrad's novella *Heart of Darkness*.

Assessment:

1. Class discussion participation grade
2. A three- to four-page written response to the prompt as writing category grade

Anticipated results:

Some students will choose to write a traditional essay of analysis. They may use some creative techniques within this framework, such as metaphoric or hyperbolic statements. Some students may write a dialogue or mini-script with two narrators communicating with each other or express the resultant miscommunication. Some students may write a detailed poem that deals with voice and theme.

In other words, as long as the student is deeply and analytically exploring the concept of the reliability of narrative and how it reveals theme, we may allow the framework or structure of the composition to be outside the graded assessment or not the focus of the assessment.

SUMMARY NOTES

Lesson plans need only be tweaked slightly to encourage students to be self-directed in creative applications of writing.

SECTION 2: TWEAKING THE ASSESSMENT RUBRIC TO ENCOURAGE CREATIVITY

These creative approaches to teaching writing involve processes with multiple drafts and formative as well as summative assessments. While incorporating these processes are time consuming, what is the cost of reaching the finishing line first if the results are weak, unintelligible, or confusingly written student compositions?

Designing a rubric for a creative approach to writing need only involve a few changes in a standard writing rubric. What is important, however, is that the student is not penalized for trying something unusual in his or her approach to the task. Scaffolding in these creative techniques will result in the greatest success, so it is important that we do not expect instantaneous results from our students.

How do we grade these creative approaches to the essay or composition? Start by being specific about what your lesson asks of students. Discuss essential and guiding questions and build your rubric around the concept(s) you want the students to learn and discover. Allow them to choose the container or framework for their ideas.

Expose them to great models that use creative approaches to writing before the workshop or writing practice. Support them in taking risks and allow them to hand in multiple drafts. Be willing to build drafting into your lesson plans.

Your rubric will be specific to your course, grade level, essential questions in your lesson plan, and the text(s), but table 15.1 is a sample from which to extract what works for your lesson and add whatever is needed to meet your lesson's objectives for student learning. The rubric is representative.

Some of the key words to incorporate involve using "development" rather than "length." A poem might be very well developed without being particularly lengthy. Certainly, creating a one-and-a-half-page poem is not equivalent to writing a one-and-a-half-page prose composition, so "length" may not be a good word for your rubric.

Focusing exactly on what you want your students to learn, providing precisely worded essential questions, and clearly communicating the parameters of the assignment allow students to then make creative choices.

Initially, we might anticipate that some students would not do as well when given creative freedom because we surmise that not everyone is inherently creative. However, we quickly discover that even the student who did not appear to be creative in other aspects of his or her academic life is, in fact, just waiting for the opportunity to discover or rediscover that creative gene.

Creating a rubric to measure creative techniques in writing or creative approaches taken allows the teacher to tailor exactly what he or she wishes to measure. The rubrics on the following pages are not meant to meet every educator's needs but simply offer a sampling of how creativity may be incorporated into a writing rubric. Table 15.2 establishes creativity as part of the grade, but the creative approach taken may also be separated, allowing teachers to measure only the final written student product.

A Sample Student Task: For your writing project, culminating our study of Toni Morrison's novel *Song of Solomon*, you will focus on the thematic concepts of character identity and the odyssey or journey of the character, as well as employ at least one literary technique. [See table 15.3.] You may choose any character, but Milkman Dead is particularly apt for this study of character and identity.

Notes to students:
Creative ideas you might consider for a writing format:

- An interview with Milkman before the end of the novel
- An epilogue to the novel in which you write an original ending
- An original poem
- A written genealogy of a character's family history with annotations

While you want to encourage students' creative choice, it is helpful to provide a few options to assist them in visualizing how such a format might work with the task of analyzing character identity, coupled with the use of a literary technique. Class discussion or writing conferences/conversations about how applications might work are also very helpful to students.

Table 15.1. Character and Journeys in *Song of Solomon* Rubric

Category	*Excellent: minimal to no errors; high level of competency*	*Mastery: few errors that do not interfere with comprehension; shows competency*	*Developing: some errors interfere with comprehension; shows some competency*	*Poor: frequent errors interfere with comprehension; minimal/ no evidence of competency*
Idea Development: thesis development and support	❑ Thesis is clear whether implicit or explicit; topic is manageable. ❑ Thesis analyzes, interprets, evaluates with minimal summary. (Summary may be implicit.) ❑ Details are relevant, interesting, vivid, and accurate; clearly support thesis.	❑ Thesis shows understanding of content and topic; has a generally clear topic. ❑ Thesis analyzes, interprets with some summary. ❑ Thesis uses details to support thesis. ❑ Thesis has minimal stray from paper's focus.	❑ Thesis is present but vague. ❑ Thesis summarizes with some analysis/ interpretation. ❑ Minimal details relate to thesis; unclear relationship to thesis. ❑ Occasionally off-topic or redundant.	❑ Thesis is unidentifiable. ❑ Thesis is mainly summary. ❑ Thesis contains irrelevant or inaccurate details; does not show relationship between details.
Organization: starts with a strong lead, builds ideas, and moves toward a thoughtful, logical conclusion	❑ Clear, purposeful introduction draws the reader in and conclusion closes essay. ❑ Strong transitions and connecting words clearly show how ideas connect. ❑ Topic sentences meaningfully develop thesis. ❑ Details fit where they're placed; logical sequencing. ❑ Writer controls pace to ensure methodical elaboration or brisk	❑ Clear introduction, body, conclusion that suit purpose of essay. ❑ Uses transitions with effectiveness; reader occasionally has to hunt for clues. ❑ Topic sentences relate to thesis. ❑ Details generally fit where placed, but some are out of place. ❑ Well-paced with some lapses in logic/ reasoning.	❑ Contains an introduction, body and conclusion. ❑ Occasionally uses transition words to aid the flow of ideas. ❑ Topic sentences do not clearly develop thesis. ❑ Some important details are out of sequence. ❑ Pacing of essay must be changed.	❑ No clear introduction, body, conclusion. ❑ Transitions show lack of control/disrupt flow of ideas. ❑ Topic sentences are out of place/do not develop thesis. ❑ Details do not fit where placed. ❑ Pacing belabors obvious points, glosses complex arguments.

Sentence Fluency: language that flows with rhythm and grace, logic and music	❑ Writing uses present tense; active sentences. ❑ Words are precise and engaging, carefully chosen. ❑ Sentences vary in length and structure and enhance/clarify meaning. ❑ Sentence structure helps clarify meaning. ❑ Sentences are concise.	❑ Writing uses consistent verb tense; largely active sentences. ❑ Words convey ideas clearly; minor problems in usage; sentences are adequate, correct. ❑ Some variety and effectiveness in sentence structure. ❑ Sentences are generally correct in structure. ❑ There are few unnecessary words.	❑ Writing has frequent shifts in tense/no use of present tense; passive voice. ❑ Words are adequate, do not get in the way, but do not enhance meaning (get, got, so, very, just). ❑ Sentences largely follow same structure/errors in variation. ❑ Some sentences sound awkward. ❑ Sentences are wordy.	❑ [illegible] improper verb tenses; passive voice. ❑ Words are trite, vague (things), do not work, are used incorrectly. ❑ Sentences follow same pattern. ❑ Sentences suffer from unnatural phrasing; are incomplete, rambling, or awkward. ❑ There are missing/excess/misplaced words.
Language Use and Conventions: includes punctuation, spelling, grammar, and usage	❑ Writing has flawless spelling, punctuation, capitalization. ❑ Correct grammar and usage add to clarity, style. ❑ Correctly uses pronoun-antecedent and subject-verb agreement. ❑ Paragraphing is sound and reinforces the organization. ❑ The writer may manipulate conventions for stylistic effect—and it works!	❑ Writing has minimal errors in spelling, punctuation, capitalization. ❑ Writing has minimal grammar/usage errors that do not detract from meaning. ❑ Writing contains some errors in agreement, but they do not interfere with meaning. ❑ There are minor problems in paragraphing; generally supports organization. ❑ Some editing is required.	❑ Writing has multiple errors in spelling, punctuation, capitalization. ❑ Some grammar/usage errors detract from meaning. ❑ Errors in agreement may hinder understanding. ❑ Paragraphing attempts to support organization but is basic. ❑ Editing is required to clarify content.	❑ Writing has frequent errors in spelling, punctuation, capitalization. ❑ Grammar/usage errors are obvious, frequent, and affect meaning. ❑ Frequent errors in agreement. ❑ Paragraphing is missing, irregular; no relationship to organization of text. ❑ Reader must read once to decode, and again for meaning; extensive editing is required.

(continued)

Table 15.1. *(Continued)*

Category	*Excellent: minimal to no errors; high level of competency*	*Mastery: few errors that do not interfere with comprehension; shows competency*	*Developing: some errors interfere with comprehension; shows some competency*	*Poor: frequent errors interfere with comprehension; minimal/ no evidence of competency*
Creativity	❑ Writing incorporates more than one creative writing strategy successfully. ❑ Student offers highly original analytical perspective. ❑ Student is self-directed in applying creative techniques to writing assignment.	❑ Writing incorporates at least one creative writing strategy successfully. ❑ Student attempts to offer original analytical perspective with varied results. ❑ Student needs some direction in applying creative techniques to writing assignment.	❑ Writing incorporates at least one creative writing strategy with varied results. ❑ Student offers clichéd perspective with weak results. ❑ Student needs close guidance to apply a creative technique to writing assignment.	❑ There is no attempt to incorporate creative writing strategies. ❑ There is no attempt by student to offer unique perspective (presenting others' ideas). ❑ Student resists teacher's efforts to guide toward application of a creative technique to a writing assignment.

Table 15.2. Creative Techniques Employed in Writing in the English Classroom

25 points per category	*Excellent: 23–25*	*Mastery: 20–22*	*Developing: 17–19*	*Poor: 14–16*
Assignment specifications	Exceeds assignment specifications in one or more categories	Meets all assignment specifications	Meets most assignment specifications with an effort to meet all requirements	No attempt to meet all specifications of the assignment or uneven application of the required specifications
Degree of creativity	Highly unusual, original, and thought-provoking application of creativity to every aspect of the assignment; demonstrates original and critical thinking	Original and creative application of every aspect of the assignment; analytical perspective is evident	Attempt to create original responses in a creative manner although the application may be uneven; one or more clichés evident	Unoriginal in style and execution; clichés evident
Execution of assignment	Flawlessly and artistically executed in every aspect	Well written	Some aspects may lack polish	Sloppy or carelessly executed assignment
Accuracy and fluency	All aspects of the project demonstrate a 100% accurate portrayal of the assignment specifications	All major aspects of the project are 100% accurate although there may be a minor error in the execution	Errors of execution but not in concept are evident	Errors in execution and concept are evident

Table 15.3. Rubric for Reader Response Writing Project for Toni Morrison's *Song of Solomon*

Category	*Score: needs work* *15–18*	*Score: good* *19–22*	*Score: excellent* *23–25*
Project specifications	Writing project shows no clear evidence of a relationship to Morrison's novel. No creative techniques are evident.	Project shows clear evidence of relationship to one or more of the novel's literary techniques and a character's identity and journey. One or more creative techniques are employed.	Project shows thoughtfully written evidence of a character's identity as well as depth in relating original ideas about Morrison's techniques. Multiple creative techniques are skillfully employed.
Project writing style	Writing project is clichéd and appears haphazard.	Writing project shows evidence of original style.	Writing project is affecting and original and shows evidence of sophistication in choices.
Accuracy	Text contains multiple errors in grammar, punctuation, usage, or interpretation.	Textual elements are largely accurate and supportable.	Textual elements are free of any errors.
Development	Project is largely undeveloped and reflects a lack of planning with scant evidence of creative techniques.	Project shows some detail in development of character identify and consideration in employing a creative technique.	Project shows careful design and in-depth, detailed analysis of character identify and technique in its execution.

16

Setting Up Action Research

SECTION 1: SURVEYS FOR ACTION RESEARCH

Every educator should want to be involved in action research as we continue to compare results of what we are doing and how we measure our students' progress through reflective practices and a systematic approach to both student evaluation and an evaluation of best practices. Taking the time to survey our students and establish a baseline composition assignment can be done at any level of teaching from the third grade up.

The survey need not be complicated or time-consuming to administer. Surveys designed to gather information about the baseline writing product and a writing product in which creative choice options are offered take only a couple of minutes of class time and can be invaluable in terms of what they may tell the teacher as well as the students. Sample surveys are incorporated here.

A higher level of engagement and interest is necessary for students' willingness to enter into the editing process where a poor composition may be improved to the point of being a good one or one that shows student mastery. Typically, students are reluctant to edit for any type of errors, whether in meaning or grammatical and mechanical errors, but students who feel invested in their product seem more willing to spend the effort to revise their writing.

While engaged students do not always correlate to higher scores on every assignment, greater levels of student interest in both the process and written product will, over time, yield improved results.

Following the administering of the surveys, teachers should build in time for writing conferences/conversations to allow students to elaborate on their survey answers and provide feedback on the assignment or specific problems in meeting the composition task. For example, writing conferences may be built into the class during discussion time while students are involved in conversations about a text, and the teacher is meeting individually with students for a few minutes before joining the circle discussions.

These conferences provide valuable feedback on the problems that students encounter with writing and what teachers can do to more efficiently and effectively help them. The grade comparison alone is not sufficient to provide the kind of information teachers and students need to make decisions about approaches to writing, although it can be used to support approaches and claims.

Teachers who build a specific framework into the assignment are inadvertently taking away the students' choice, and the results showing improvement will probably not be as significant as those assignments in which student preference is built into the task and scoring rubric.

Some students may do their best work and feel invested in an essay that strictly follows a pyramid structure for a five-paragraph essay, but for the many students who feel that the strictures limit their ability to deeply and critically explore a topic, the creative choice option removes a barrier before takeoff.

The following two student surveys may be helpful by way of example in beginning action research in your own classroom.

Name: ______________________________ Date: ________

Specify your level of engagement and interest in this writing project by placing a checkmark in the box that most accurately reflects the nature of your engagement with this assignment.

Categories	**Sporadic or little to none** ✓	**Following directions and meeting minimum requirements** ✓	**Owning my project and highly involved** ✓
Level of engagement or interest in this writing project			
Investment of time in the written product			
Level of editing and revising			

Baseline composition grade: ______

Name: ______________________________ Date: ________

Specify your level of engagement and interest in this writing project by placing a checkmark in the box that most accurately reflects the nature of your engagement with this assignment.

Categories	**Sporadic or little to none** ✓	**Following directions and meeting minimum requirements** ✓	**Owning my project and highly involved** ✓
Level of engagement or interest in this writing project			
Investment of time in the written product			
Level of editing and revising			

Creative choice option, writing assignment grade: _______ Baseline composition: _______

SECTION 2: EXAMINING COMPARATIVE DATA

An example of one teacher research project follows:

Why this summative assessment was chosen for the APPR (Annual Professional Performance Review):
This summative assessment requires student involvement and engagement at all of the most rigorous levels of Bloom's Taxonomy, the new critical thinking rubric that includes a greater level of self-direction on the students' part as well as a higher level of creativity.

It is designed to be challenging and helpful to students in their efforts to become more independent in making the choices involved in academic writing—moving toward true scholarship—while simultaneously encouraging students to become more creative in their writing applications.

Rigors of the assignment and how it meets the higher realm in Bloom's Taxonomy:
This assignment and assessment require students to critically think, plan, evaluate, analyze, read, apply their understandings, acquire new knowledge, and create original works of poetry/prose, exemplifying the highest realms in Bloom's revised Taxonomy, as well as incorporates our district's new Critical Thinking rubrics. Creativity and self-direction, specifically, were singled out and measured through the assessment process on the rubric.

Critical thinking aspects of Bloom's Taxonomy, incorporated into the lesson and writing tasks:
Students were asked to INTERPRET and APPLY their knowledge of writing techniques (allusion, symbolism, alliteration, metaphor, and narrative techniques in poetry) in Eliot's poem, choose a creative approach or application to bring to their literary analysis, demonstrate understanding of a difficult work of literature (Eliot's seminal poem), and ANALYZE information found in the poem and class discussions, following the research they conducted.

This project required careful examination of the literature, questioning, and hypothesizing about the work, the poem, and the subject matter of the literature.

Anecdotal analysis of the comparison between the baseline assignment and the summative assessment:
Self-direction and deadlines:
Every student handed in his or her summative assessment paper on time. This was not the case with the baseline assignment. Three students handed in late papers on the first assignment although late points were taken out of the equation for comparative purposes. The fact that every student handed in a paper in itself points to a higher level of student involvement in the creative analysis writing project.

Table 16.1. Comparative Data Analysis, AP English Block 2, Days 2 and 4

Student Identification Code	*Grade on Baseline Essay*	*Following creative techniques instruction and modeling: Grade on writing assignment (of comparative page requirement length, time length to complete the assignment, and thematic complexity) with creative choice*	*Point Differential*
Student A	70	95	+25
Student B	81	91	+10
Student C	83	100	+17
Student G	84	94	+10
Student H	80	94	+14
Student I	84	92	+8
Student J	88	100	+12
Student K	73	94	+21
Student L	82	92	+10
Student M	N/A (She entered the class from another school mid-marking period)	90	N/A
Student N	83	93	+10
Student O	90	100	+10
Student P	74	86	+12
Student Q	87	100	+13

Completing the challenge:
Students who seldom, if ever, take risks with their writing took a leap and found their efforts rewarded through superior products and improved grades on the summative assessment. All students in the AP English class applied at least one creative technique and most applications were stunningly creative.

The overall quality of their summative paper analyses was significantly more sophisticated and more intriguingly articulated than that found in the baseline papers.

Grammar and mechanics:
There were fewer grammatical and mechanical errors in the group of summative assessment papers as a whole than those found in the baseline essays. While there are other variables at work here, including direct instruction in grammar, the fact that the students retained this information and applied it correctly in their summative assessments is clear.

Regarding the surveys:
Although many of the students checked the same category in the time spent editing, there is very clear evidence of an improvement in the number of grammatical and mechanical problems from the baseline to the summative assessment paper. What accounts for this variable?

While students may not always be able to consciously reflect on the correlation between the time spent editing and improved results, the papers and grades demonstrate one such correlation in this project.

Improved grades on a more difficult task:
Every single student in the AP English Literature and Composition class saw a significant improvement in grade (as well as quality of writing) from the baseline essay to the summative assessment essay. Interestingly enough, the summative assessment paper was a much more difficult task, given with far greater time constraints (one weekend as opposed to the entire summer for the baseline essay).

Student engagement:
Another intriguing result of the data examination is that every student marked the high-interest category on the summative assessment except one, and that student chose not to take a particularly creative approach. She struggled with applying a creative technique and needed additional prompting.

In spite of that difficulty, however, she showed a marked improvement in grammar and mechanics on the summative assessment, resulting in a twelve-point increase in her grade from her baseline essay. Perhaps it was just the additional time in which she struggled to be creative that allowed her to discover some of her errors in grammar and mechanics.

Summary of the test data (see table 16.1):

- Thirteen of fourteen students improved their grades from the baseline essay to the summative writing project. The fourteenth student did not write the baseline essay because she came into this class mid-marking period from another school. Therefore, 100 percent of the students who wrote the baseline essay and summative essay improved their grades.
- The average increase was 12.90 or 13 points.
- The average grade for students on this assessment was 94.36. The average grade for students on the baseline essay was 81.46.
- Both the physical data and the anecdotal information clearly show a dramatic increase in student performance, better student comprehension, deeper understanding of the material, and superior student application of the skills as well as the lesson's objectives.
- When given permission to try creative approaches in writing, this group of students responded positively and challenged themselves in a self-directed manner with excellent results.

Variables:

- Timeline—the baseline essay assignment parameters gave students more time to complete the writing assignment. We would anticipate that the assignment that allowed more time would generate the higher grade, but the opposite proved to be true.

- Mechanics and grammar—students received direct instruction in grammar and mechanics following the baseline essay formative assessment.
- Material—the baseline essay task was significantly easier in the sense that it was more familiar to students. Familiarity does not necessarily equate to successful completion of writing tasks.
- Student population—although the same students wrote the baseline and summative assessments, this group of AP English Literature and Composition students tends to perform at the highest academic levels in the school. Therefore, a project in which they were allowed greater flexibility, freedom, and creative choice might be seen as a natural fit for more motivated students.

This research has been conducted in other classes, in addition to the one discussed in this chapter, with similar results.

SUMMARY NOTES

Any teacher can conduct action research, using repeatable procedures, and examine the data in order to help students improve their writing.

SECTION 3: A PROCEDURAL GUIDE TO BUILDING CREATIVE CHOICE INTO THE COMPOSITIONAL ASSIGNMENT

Procedures for building creative choice into the writing assignment are outlined here:

1. Baseline essay or composition assignment
2. Student survey following completion of the baseline assignment
3. Writing conferences with students to discuss student's time investment and engagement with the writing
4. Instruction in specific, creative technique
5. Introduction of models of good writing using creative techniques
6. Class discussions on the techniques employed by the writers
7. Activities centered on practicing or identifying the techniques
8. Short writing assignments to explore students' use of a technique in meeting a lesson goal
9. Lesson on a text or topic
10. Essential and guiding questions of the lesson discussed
11. Writing task that allows for creative choice in framework and implementation of the task

12. Writing process with drafting and mini-conferences with students before final drafting
13. Writing product assessed
14. Post-writing survey administered
15. Mini-conferences on writing following surveys and results

While the number of steps may seem daunting in terms of class time at first, several of them may be combined with other activities going on in class. For example, mini-conferences may take place simultaneously with other classroom activities. Drafting may take place in or outside of class time. Surveys may be completed during class or as homework.

If we can help our students to become better writers, the time investment is well worth it. Saving time in the classroom is no savings if our students' written products do not improve or reflect the complexity of their thoughts.

SUMMARY NOTES

Teaching creative techniques and encouraging creative choice to improve student writing are repeatable instructional practices that will engender positive results in student writing.

17

Providing Students with Opportunities for an Authentic Audience

It has been well documented that students will take greater ownership of their written products if there is an opportunity for an authentic audience. The teacher as the only member of the audience for the student becomes repetitive and, in many cases, lacking in meaning for a young writer.

Elementary teachers have long done a good job of providing these creative opportunities, as any visitor can see by strolling through an elementary school. The children and visitors see student work on the classroom walls, in the hallways, on bulletin boards, in class books, and in grade-level publications.

Something happens, however, when a child enters high school. The rigors of a multitude of courses, the workload on students and teachers, and the nonteaching demands on teachers' time begin to impact the opportunities a teacher is able to make available for an authentic audience. While we are aware that publication should be a part of every student's educational experience, finding the time in the day to make this possible seems daunting.

This is not to say that high school teachers do not seek to help students find a larger readership for their written work, however. There are certainly examples in secondary schools of exemplary publications in which some students' works are featured and widely read, but those opportunities tend to be reserved for elite writers or for only a fairly small percentage of students in each school.

This is one area where parents as well as teachers can be tremendously helpful. By screening sources and compiling a list of writing contests—both online and print publications—teachers and parents can encourage their children to submit their written work and seek an authentic audience.

There are more writing contests available on the Internet than ever before. We should be wary, however, of money-making schemes in which the contest entrant has to pay large fees or purchase a product. The *Writer's Market* is a text that provides thousands of lists for contests, publishers, magazines, journals, and more.

Academic summer camps and seminars in writing that take place on college and university campuses offer both instruction and opportunities for feedback from other students and professional writers and instructors.

Teachers may share information about contests and student sites located on the Web with their classes. Using a blackboard or corner of the classroom to post news about writing contests is one way of encouraging students to seek an authentic audience.

It is also possible to become a curator of a classroom site on the National Gallery of Writing, screening student products for publication globally. In addition, countless teachers maintain Web pages where students' works are published.

You may want to work across the curriculum with colleagues in other departments to provide unique publishing opportunities for your students. It is amazing the resources we have in our own colleagues. Members of high school art departments may work very well with members of English departments to create these types of avenues for our students.

On a number of occasions, we have planned out and jointly produced our school literary magazine with outstanding results.

Instructional Application and Dedication

What follows is an application of creative techniques that are incorporated in the educational text as instructional tools used to examine literary movements and as a dedication to my students.

English Class
Post-Modernism
As their teacher,
I have become accomplished
at reading the refracted images
revealed as individuals,
paradoxically both
idiosyncratic and adumbrative,
approaching the present
moment, wary of Faulkner's
nonexistent future
colliding with
the here and now
in our classroom,
these young men
and women about to survey
the literary landscape,
through their distinctive
visible aspects, as
self-consciously but not nearly
as self-reflexively as
their teacher.

Empiricism
Sara enters wearing
her scarf, resembling
a Sonya Macintosh
kelp creation rather
than mere clothing
swirling about her neck,
her one bare shoulder
suggesting overt sexuality
while her open-mouthed smile,
still moist from that kiss in the
hallway, argues about everything
that she has not seen or,
more importantly, felt
with the tips of her slender
fingers; she demands
knowledge derived
from sensory experience
in the way she knows the distance
to the boy in the leather jacket
by the measure of
her long lashes brushing
his still silky cheek.

Transgressive
John's poem on
the color of debauchery
experienced the night before,
just one instance
of his pushing
boundaries beyond
apology;
John designing shock
like strident chords
in a Stravinsky fugue,
seemingly difficult
and discordant,
his brilliance cloaked by
self-effacing commentary,
rhythmic in phrasing,
his brown curly hair cropped
short and his slight
build covered by
clothing purposely
nondescript, nothing
cool about him but
his punishing, original,
and transgressive wit.

Confessional
Mara, pushing her
glasses up the bridge
of her nose, pulls her
thin brown hair
behind her elfin ears,
bleeds in her poems
and journal entries,
non-metaphorically cutting
her arms then covering
those white birch limbs
in fear or shame or both,
powerlessness taking
control like Plath
in "Daddy," defiantly
remarking without
opening her mouth,
her pen
whispering rather
than screaming,
I'm through,
I'm through.

Literary Minimalism
Sahar is a literary
minimalist,
answering with a
single word or
the angle of his
head when the
occasion calls
for analysis;
he asks only,
"Why?"
stating
that he really
doesn't care
even when he's
trying not to cry,
and he's called
to the office,
rolling his eyes,
so the sclera
startles.

Absolutism
Denise remains resolute
in her belief that

what is morally
wrong with the world
is absolute
and unconditional,
arguing with
her scathing irony
on display
in her essays
and journalistic
endeavors,
leading by
example and
a self-assurance,
emphatically
stating
the mind and body,
born of fear and anxiety,
are also aspects of
imagination: this
enlightened, young,
imaginary monarch.

Transcendentalism
Greg, with his untamed
hair, poet's shirt, and
bright orange pants,
finds his center while
reading Thoreau's *Walden;*
preferring the
uncorrupted,
the natural,
he is self-reliant,
self-confident,
and could hold
rational discourse
with the members
of the Saturday Morning
Club at the Omni Hotel,
if such an exclusive
society of intellectuals
still existed, he
muses, scarcely
realizing that he
is flamboyantly
channeling Whitman.

Idealism
Quiet, serious Sam,
whose mother
died during
the school year,
shoulders
responsibility
and exactness,
the essay in his
notebook unwilling
to be exposed
before editing,
before becoming
a model to
awe even the skeptical
student,
the lyricism
a breathtaking surprise
inherent
in the perfect
analysis.

Gothic
Draped in a tall coat,
resembling an opera cape,
Matt, a pseudo-vampire,
colors his nails black,
paints his eyes with
charcoal eyeliner, dyes
his blonde hair the color
of a raven's feathers, and
cloaks himself
in self-immolating
alienation,
composing
the story
as he goes,
one shadowy anti-hero
after another
exacting revenge
on the bullies
of his imaginings,
all too familiar
in the dark hallways.

Dark Romanticism
Keshia has novels in
progress, she tells me,
nothing finished
or complete,
but her words
reveal the
sustained tension
between male
and female, the insatiable
passion, as her characters
circle about the room as
recognizable wolves,
changelings,
and handsome young men,
somewhat dangerous,
waiting at the wings, while the
heroine reveals
the strange power
in her always
amethyst-colored
eyes.

Oulipo
Steve's journal
reads better than
a novel, the letters
straining, nearly spilling
off the page, palindromes
of dam(n) mad men
trapped by Calvino-
inspired constraints,
his scrawl nearly
indecipherable but
nevertheless revelatory,
the boy, whose father
walked out on him when
he was three,
finding his way to
manhood with the
stops and starts of
the pen's ink,
the author's original
voice cast in the angst
masked as
cockiness.

Skepticism
Battling
Asperger syndrome,
Raymond dismisses any
statement his experience
does not underscore,
using erudite vocabulary
unfamiliar to the rest
of the class, he
hesitates a moment,
not quite stuttering,
before launching
into a monologue,
literal rather than figurative,
that insightfully enlightens,
challenges the expected,
words flowing so quickly
quick . . . quick . . . quickly
that the language suddenly
jams, and he stops
momentarily,
paradoxically
poetic.

Beat
Soft-spoken,
dark-eyed
Mark plays
percussion
in the classroom
as well as on the stage,
drumming out a
Kerouac beat that
repeats the rhythm we
feel as well
as hear when he
speaks, writes,
composes,
providing *Hamlet*'s
Ophelia
with her own
xylophone concerto,
striking the shorter
bars to indicate
her high-pitched
madness,
burying
his own
sadness.

Modernism
Ellen
with no trace
of
lilt to her voice still
suggests her Irish
heritage,
linking her
to Beckett and Yeats,
experimenting
with structure as much as language
content,
as we ferret the Gaelic influence
out of the English writings of Joyce;

she suggests we continue to correspond
long after she has graduated,
this student
of literature
and
the heart,
the heart, the
heart.

Realism
Claire, who sees clear-eyed
with her glasses on,
informs me that
literature is not her thing;
science and mathematics
come easily for her.
She is certain, however,
that she will attain
competency, if not
mastery, in order
to pass all required tests
and experience the challenge
and rigor of the AP
English literature course
without Henry James
to contend with
because James
is a bore by
her detailed,
uncompromising
equations.

Stream of Consciousness
Zamid says that he can't think today because he is too
tired to think and was wondering if he could just get a drink,
Miss, from the machine in the hallway then he was wondering if
he could talk to his guidance counselor or maybe go to the
lav because why do they call it a rest room if you don't rest in there
he couldn't concentrate on a day like this what kind of day? he repeats
—don't know—you ask too many questions, Miss, he says responding
before the black analog clock has ticked off a minute—only one minute?
he just needs to get a little sleep because if he can't then
he can't think so what's the point of coming to school but this
good-looking girl smiled at him this morning so that's the point
he guesses

Magic Realism
Christie has
transformed herself
from a serious and good
student to an exceptional scholar
and poet. In the process,
she's become
a she-wolf,
quietly lapping
at the water
in the riverbed,
a brief respite
from pursuing
the language down
the steep slope
where she will
wait in the quiet
of the morning
before the doe
emerges from
the forest.

Imagism
The actress whose
passion comes alive
at center stage, Brienne
sees the world in
images, interwoven
complex metaphors—
Alice and the White
Rabbit sliding down into
a realm of the tenuous

atmosphere of
imagination,
Brienne playing
the part of the
Red Queen
as much for
the character's color
and fervency
as her strident lines;
beautiful Brienne
breathes one blue
image after a
red image after a
blue one.

Existentialism
Alec, whose older
sister was a top student,
contends that
everything is a
placeholder for
possibility,
so Beckett's
Godot might,
in fact, appear
as almost anyone
or anything, whether
or not we accept
the speculation
or faith that
Godot is somehow
hope or God
or just the landlord
who owns the
real estate on
which we are
inconveniently
parked.

Post-Modernism Redux
At the doorway,
I observe them swimming
against the current, with the current,
leaping out of the stream entirely,
a few gasping on the bank,

moving in this watery conceit,
discerning the underlying
order in the seemingly random
design until the bell rings
and then, switching metaphors,
conspicuously and consciously
articulated like bees, they swarm
for the hive, laughing, buzzing,
cursing, muttering, suddenly
silent again, sullen, disaffected,
or profoundly in love,
as I open the door
to the tumult, realizing
what I see in all of them
are their possibilities.

Appendix A: A Guide for Parents

While parents will not be involved in writing the curricula or the assignments, they can be active in helping their children become better writers. Here are a few suggestions that should prove to be highly effective:

- Provide opportunities for reading and support reading in the home by being a reader yourself and modeling for your child. Read anything. Make your child's access to books easy by going to the library, using online sources, and using personal technology (such as the Kindle) to expand a child's library. Purchase books for gifts. The relationship between good writing and extensive reading is a direct one and well documented.
- Ask about the essential questions of the writing assignment. These are the most important questions at the heart of the lesson. They should be open ended, allowing for discussion, questioning, and reframing of answers. Any question that can be answered with a "yes" or "no" answer is not an essential question.
- Discuss the topic with and listen to your child's ideas before offering your own suggestions. It is tempting to provide the solution when your child is struggling with a lesson, an assignment, or an idea, but progress in writing and as a critical thinker comes from within. The struggle is an important part of the process, so allow your child that time to work through the difficulties.
- Ask your child how he/she plans to approach the assignment. Don't offer application suggestions unless your child asks for help.

- If you can find the time, write with your child even if it is totally unrelated written work. If your child needs help in coming up with approaches, discuss with him or her the creative frameworks provided in this text. Remember, the choice needs to be owned by your child.
- Show support for your child's writing risk-taking even if the assessment/grade is not what is desired. The grades will improve over time. Value the process, the thinking, and the learning more than the grade.
- Help your child find good models of creative approaches and creative techniques in excellent writing in the books your child has already read.
- Ask your child what error in grammar or mechanics is being focused on in the editing process.
- Follow up with your child about errors in grammar and mechanics in subsequent writing assignments. This should not be punitive but rather like a puzzle. What piece was discovered? Did he or she reduce the type of error already identified by the teacher or your child? Ask your child what strategies he or she uses to find errors in writing.
- Stay interested in your child's development as a writer even when the improvements seem to be slow in coming. Significant improvement in writing takes time, your child's willingness to try new techniques, and practice.

Appendix B: A Sampling of Young Writers' Conferences

Look for a writers' workshop program at your nearest college or university.

- **Bread Loaf** is one of the most well-known and well-respected young writers' conferences. New England Young Writers' Conference (NEYWC) is typically scheduled in May. The application process for the conference begins in the fall.
  To apply to attend Bread Loaf, contact:
  New England Young Writers' Conference
  212 Adirondack House
  Middlebury College
  Middlebury, VT 05753
  (802) 443-3071
  neywc@middlebury.edu
- **California Writing Project (CWP): Young Writers' Camps**
  For more information about one in your area of California, visit CWP's Website:
  www.californiawritingproject.org/Parents/young_writers_camps.html
- **Champlain College Young Writers' Conference** offers a residential, weekend experience in Burlington, Vermont.
  For more information, contact:
  Lesley Wright, CCYW Coordinator
  588 Fern Lake Road
  Leicester, VT 05733
  (802) 247-5920
  ccyw@champlain.edu

- **Hood College** offers summer conferences for young writers.
  For more information, contact:
  Hood College
  401 Rosemont Ave.
  Frederick, MD 21701
  (301) 663-3131
- **Iowa Young Writers' Studio**
  The University of Iowa has one of the best writing programs in the world at the undergraduate as well as graduate school levels.
  For more information, contact:
  Iowa Young Writers' Studio
  The University of Iowa
  C215 Seashore Hall
  Iowa City, IA 52242-1402
  (319) 335-4209
- **New Pages.com** on the Web posts lists of opportunities for summer writing conferences that are updated continually.
  For more information, go to the NewPages Website:
  www.newpages.com/writing-conferences
- **New York University** offers an amazing program called Writers in Paris in the summers for high school students.
  For more information, contact:
  Deborah Landau, Program Director
  (212) 998-8816
  writers.in.paris@nyu.edu
- **Southern Illinois University Carbondale** annually hosts a Young Writers' Workshop.
  For more information, contact:
  Division of Continuing Education, Mail Code 6705
  Washington Square C, Southern Illinois University
  Carbondale, IL 62901-6705
- **Susquehanna University** in Belingsgrove, Pennsylvania, holds a Writing Action Day for high school students visiting the campus. This university also offers summer workshops for high school students.
  For more information on these programs, contact:
  Office of Admissions
  (570) 372-4260
  1-800-326-9672
  suadmiss@susqu.edu
- **University of Virginia (UVA)** annually hosts the UVA Young Writers' Workshop.
  For more information, e-mail *your name and e-mail address* to:
  writers@virginia.edu

There are young writers' workshops offered at nearly every major university and college in the country, and an educational institution of higher learning is a good source for providing this type of instruction. Be wary of the numerous online workshops offered by individuals who may charge excessive fees without necessarily having the expertise.

Appendix C: Helpful, Creative Resources for Writers and Writing Instruction

- Annie Dillard's *The Writing Life*, published by Harper & Row, Inc., 1989.
  The one book you will want to carry everywhere with you as a reader and writer.
- Natalie Goldberg's *Writing Down the Bones: Freeing the Writer Within*, published by Shambhala, 2010.
- Danny Gregory's *An Illustrated Life: Drawing Inspiration from the Private Sketchbooks of Artists, Illustrators and Designers*, published by How Books, F&W Publications, 2008.
  This collection of journal entries and words by artists and writers offers a look at the journey of the creative process for visual and print media artists. It is hard to read this book and look at the illustrations without wanting to start a journal.
- Judith Kitchen and Mary Paumier Jones's edited work *In Short: A Collection of Brief Creative Nonfiction*, published by W. W. Norton, New York, 1996.
  This work offers creative nonfiction models for both students and writing instructors.
- Matt Madden's *99 Ways to Tell a Story: Exercises in Style*, published by Chamberlain Bros., a member of Penguin Group, Inc., New York, 2005.
  This amazingly clever illustrated book helps students understand, visualize, analyze the effects of, and play with various points of view as well as narrative formats.

- Sam Seidel's *Hip Hop Genius*, published by Rowman & Littlefield Education, 2011.
  Seidel's text is immensely creative in its approach to education, asking instructors to consider some vastly different ideas in terms of how we offer education, particularly to students who have their own creative ideas about how to proceed, only waiting for opportunities to express them.
- *Teaching Writing Creatively*, edited by David Starkey, published by Boynton/Cook, 1998.

Notes

PREFACE

1. David Bartholomae, *Writing on the Margins: Essays on Composition and Teaching* (New York: Bedford St. Martin's, 2005), 68.
2. Bartholomae, *Writing on the Margins*, 37.
3. Annie Dillard, *The Writing Life* (New York: Harper & Row, 1989), 78.
4. Roger Rosenblatt, "The Writer as Detective," *New York Times*, Sunday Section, July 8, 2011: 27.
5. Virginia Woolf, "The Modern Essay," chapter 19, *The Common Reader* (eBooks@Adelaide, University of Adelaide, August 24, 2010, updated April 29, 2012), ebooks.adelaide.edu.au/w/woolf/virginia/w91c/chapter19.html.
6. Maria Antoniou and Jessica Moriarty, "What Can Academic Writers Learn from Creative Writers? Developing Guidance and Support for Lecturers in Higher Education," *Teaching in Higher Education* 13, no. 2 (2008): 157–67.
7. Bartholomae, *Writing on the Margins*, 37.
8. Malcolm Gladwell, *Blink: The Power of Thinking without Thinking* (New York: Little Brown and Company, 2005), 276.

CHAPTER 1

1. Dan Beachy-Quick, *A Whaler's Dictionary* (Minneapolis: Milkweed Editions, 2008).
2. David Foster Wallace, "Tense Present: Democracy, English, and the Wars over Usage," in *Critical Encounters with Texts: Finding a Place to Stand*, ed. Margaret Himley and Anne Fitzsimmons (Boston: Pearson Custom Publishing, 2004), 539–41.

3. Pico Iyer, "In Praise of the Humble Comma," in *Critical Encounters with Texts*, 285.
4. Wallace, "Tense Present," 545.
5. Iyer, "In Praise of the Humble Comma," 287.
6. Conrad Aiken, "The Room," *Selected Poems* (Oxford: Oxford University Press, 1952), l. 23.
7. Samuel Johnson, "The Critic," *The Idler*, no. 60 (June 9, 1759), www.ourcivilisation.com/smartboard/shop/johnsons/idler/chap60.htm.
8. Maria Antoniou and Jessica Moriarty, "What Can Academic Writers Learn From Creative Writers? Developing Guidance and Support for Lecturers in Higher Education," *Teaching in Higher Education* 13, no. 2 (2008): 157–67.
9. Students' names used in this text are pseudonyms if followed by an asterisk. All students gave oral and written permission for the writing excerpts included here to be published in whole or in part.

CHAPTER 2

1. Peter Elbow, *Writing with Power: Techniques for Mastering the Writing Process*, New Edition (New York/Oxford: Oxford University Press, 1998), 61.
2. Virginia Woolf, "The Modern Essay," chapter 19, *The Common Reader* (eBooks@Adelaide, University of Adelaide, August 24, 2010, updated April 29, 2012), ebooks.adelaide.edu.au/w/woolf/virginia/w91c/chapter19.html, ¶ 8.
3. Samuel Beckett, *Worstward Ho*, Samuel Beckett On-line Resources and Links Pages, Earthlink, accessed June 2012, www.samuel-beckett.net/w_ho.htm.
4. Elbow, introduction to *Writing with Power*, xix.
5. Alvin Toffler and John Hennessey, "Embracing the Need to Learn and Relearn," President's Column, *Stanford Magazine*, January/February 2002, accessed August 8 2002, alumni.stanford.edu/get/page/magazine/article/?article_id=38371.
6. Bruce Pirie, *Reshaping High School English* (Urbana, IL: National Council of Teachers of English, 1997), 86.

CHAPTER 3

1. Walter Wellesley "Red" Smith, Quote Investigator, September 14, 2011, accessed January 21, 2012, quoteinvestigator.com/2011/09/14/writing-bleed.
2. Michael Depp, "On Essays: Literature's Most Misunderstood Form," *Poets & Writers* 30, no. 4 (July/August 2002): 1, www.pw.org/content/essays?cmnt_all=1.
3. David Mamet, "Secret Names," in *The Best American Nonrequired Reading*, ed. Dave Eggers (Boston: Houghton Mifflin Harcourt, 2004), 260.
4. Peter Elbow, *Writing with Power: Techniques for Mastering the Writing Process*, New Edition (New York/Oxford: Oxford University Press, 1998).
5. Bruce Pirie, *Reshaping High School English* (Urbana, IL: National Council of Teachers of English, 1997), 76.
6. Robyn R. Jackson, "Moving from Individualization to Customization," Mindsteps Inc., 2009, mindstepsinc.com/dlresources/protected/Customization.pdf.
7. Jackson, "Moving from Individualization to Customization."

8. Elbow, *Writing with Power*, 8.

9. David Bartholomae, *Writing on the Margins: Essays on Composition and Teaching* (New York: Bedford St. Martin's, 2005), 123.

10. Elbow, introduction to *Writing with Power*, xxiv.

11. Alison Zmuda, "Springing into Active Learning," *ASCD Journal* 66, no. 3 (2008): 38–42.

12. Elbow, *Writing with Power*, 18.

13. David Jauss, "Who's Afraid of the Big Bad Abstraction? Modes of Conveying Emotion," *The Writer's Chronicle* (Association of Writers & Writing Programs [AWP]) 44, no. 6 (May/Summer 2012): 73.

CHAPTER 4

1. Annie Proulx, "Inspiration? Head Down the Back Road, and Stop for the Yard Sales," *The New York Times*, May 10, 1999, accessed June 12, 2012, partners.nytimes.com/library/books/051099proulx-writing.html, ¶ 2.

2. Larry Johnson and Annette Lamb, "Critical and Creative Thinking—Bloom's Taxonomy," 2000–2011, eduscapes.com/tap/topic69.htm.

3. Mark Doty, "Souls on Ice," in *Introspections: Contemporary American Poets on One of Their Own Poems*, ed. Robert Pack and Jay Parini, 1 (Middlebury, VT: Middlebury College Press, 1997), accessed May 15, 2012, from American Academy of Poets, www.poets.org/viewmedia.php/prmMID/15847.

4. David Jauss, "Who's Afraid of the Big Bad Abstraction? Modes of Conveying Emotion," *The Writer's Chronicle* (Association of Writers & Writing Programs [AWP]) 44, no. 6 (May/Summer 2012): 73.

5. Jauss, "Who's Afraid of the Big Bad Abstraction?" 73.

6. Annie Dillard, *The Writing Life* (New York: Harper & Row, 1989), 52.

7. Peter Elbow, introduction to *Writing with Power: Techniques for Mastering the Writing Process*, New Edition (New York/Oxford: Oxford University Press, 1998), xviii.

8. Elbow, introduction to *Writing with Power*, xxv.

9. Mark Doty, "Souls on Ice," 1.

CHAPTER 6

1. T. S. Eliot, "Marie Lloyd," 1922, in *The Selected Prose of T. S. Eliot*, ed. Frank Kermode (New York: Farrar, 1975), 172–74.

CHAPTER 7

1. Henry Hitchings, *The Secret Life of Words: How English Became English* (New York: Farrar, Straus and Giroux, 2008), 6.

2. Bruce Pirie, *Reshaping High School English* (Urbana, IL: National Council of Teachers of English, 1997), 88.

3. Henry David Thoreau. Chapter 2 of *Walden*, 156.

4. Annie Dillard, "Living Like Weasels," *Teaching a Stone to Talk*, 2.
5. Henry David Thoreau. Chapter 2 of *Walden*, 150.
6. Henry David Thoreau. Chapter 2 of *Walden*, 150.
7. Henry David Thoreau. Chapter 2 of *Walden*, 150.
8. Henry David Thoreau. Chapter 2 of *Walden*, 157.
9. Henry David Thoreau. Chapter 2 of *Walden*, 160.
10. Annie Dillard, "Living Like Weasels," 5.

CHAPTER 9

1. Virginia Woolf, "The Modern Essay," chapter 19, *The Common Reader* (eBooks@Adelaide, University of Adelaide, August 24, 2010, updated April 29, 2012), ebooks.adelaide.edu.au/w/woolf/virginia/w91c/chapter19.html.
2. Flannery O'Connor, "The Nature and Aim of Fiction," in *Mystery and Manners, Occasional Prose*, ed. Sally Fitzgerald and Robert Fitzgerald (New York: Farrar, Straus and Giroux, 1969, 26th printing, 2000), 77.
3. Danny Gregory, *An Illustrated Life* (Cincinnati: How Books, 2008), 19, 7, 34, 43.
4. Christopher Hitchens, "Unspoken Truths," *Vanity Fair* (June 2011): 95.
5. Bruce Pirie, *Reshaping High School English* (Urbana, IL: National Council of Teachers of English, 1997), 82.

CHAPTER 11

1. Allison Zmuda, "Springing into Active Learning," *ASCD Journal* 66, no. 3 (2008): ¶ 25, 38–42.

CHAPTER 12

1. Peter Elbow, *Writing with Power: Techniques for Mastering the Writing Process*, New Edition (New York/Oxford: Oxford University Press, 1998), 276.
2. David Bartholomae, *Writing on the Margins: Essays on Composition and Teaching* (New York: Bedford St. Martin's, 2005), 50.
3. Danny Gregory, *An Illustrated Life* (Cincinnati: How Books, 2008), 5.

CHAPTER 13

1. Stephen King, Goodreads.com, accessed June 2011, www.goodreads.com/quotes/65360-write-with-the-door-closed-rewrite-with-the-door-open.
2. Stephen King, ThinkExist.com, accessed May 2011, thinkexist.com/quotation/talent_is_cheaper_than_table_salt-what_separates/220123.html.
3. Annie Dillard, *The Writing Life* (New York: Harper & Row, 1989), 75.
4. David Bartholomae, *Writing on the Margins: Essays on Composition and Teaching* (New York: Bedford St. Martin's, 2005), 48.

Bibliography

Aiken, Conrad. "The Room." *Selected Poems*. Oxford: Oxford University Press, 1952.

Antoniou, Maria, and Jessica Moriarty. "What Can Academic Writers Learn from Creative Writers? Developing Guidance and Support for Lecturers in Higher Education." *Teaching in Higher Education* 13, no. 2 (2008).

Bartholomae, David. *Writing on the Margins: Essays on Composition and Teaching*. New York: Bedford St. Martin's, 2005.

Beachy-Quick, Dan. *A Whaler's Dictionary*. Minneapolis: Milkweed Editions, 2008.

Beckett, Samuel. *Worstward Ho*. Samuel Beckett On-line Resources and Links Pages, EarthLink. Accessed June 2012, www.samuel-beckett.net/w_ho.htm.

Depp, Michael. "On Essays: Literature's Most Misunderstood Form." *Poets & Writers* 30, no. 4 (July/August 2002). www.pw.org/content/essays?cmnt_all=1.

Dillard, Annie. "Living Like Weasels." *Teaching a Stone to Talk: Expeditions and Encounters*. New York: Harper & Row.

Dillard, Annie. *The Writing Life*. New York: Harper & Row, 1989.

Doty, Mark. "Souls on Ice." In *Introspections: Contemporary American Poets on One of Their Own Poems*. Ed. Robert Pack and Jay Parini, 1. Middlebury, VT: Middlebury College Press, 1997. Accessed May 15, 2012, from American Academy of Poets, www.poets.org/viewmedia.php/prmMID/15847.

Elbow, Peter. *Writing with Power: Techniques for Mastering the Writing Process*. New Edition. New York/Oxford: Oxford University Press, 1998.

Eliot, T. S. "Marie Lloyd." 1922. In *The Selected Prose of T. S. Eliot*. Ed. Frank Kermode, 172–74. New York: Farrar, 1975.

Gladwell, Malcolm. *Blink: The Power of Thinking without Thinking*. New York: Little Brown and Company, 2005.

Gregory, Danny. *An Illustrated Life*. Cincinnati: How Books, 2008.

Hitchens, Christopher. "Unspoken Truths." *Vanity Fair* (June 2011): 95.

Hitchings, Henry. *The Secret Life of Words: How English Became English*. New York: Farrar, Strauss and Giroux, 2008.

Iyer, Pico. "In Praise of the Humble Comma." In *Critical Encounters with Texts: Finding a Place to Stand*. Ed. Margaret Himley and Anne Fitzsimmons. Boston: Pearson Custom Publishing, 2004.

Jackson, Robyn. R. "Moving from Individualization to Customization." Mindsteps Inc., 2009. mindstepsinc.com/dlresources/protected/Customization.pdf.

Jauss, David. "Who's Afraid of the Big Bad Abstraction? Modes of Conveying Emotion." *The Writer's Chronicle* (Association of Writers & Writing Programs [AWP]) 44, no. 6. (May/Summer 2012): 64–79.

Johnson, Larry, and Annette Lamb. "Critical and Creative Thinking—Bloom's Taxonomy," 2000–2011. eduscapes.com/tap/topic69.htm.

Johnson, Samuel. "The Critic," *The Idler*, no. 60 (June 9, 1759). www.ourcivilisation.com/smartboard/shop/johnsons/idler/chap60.htm.

King, Stephen. Goodreads.com. Accessed June 2011, www.goodreads.com/quotes/65360-write-with-the-door-closed-rewrite-with-the-door-open.

King, Stephen. ThinkExist.com. Accessed May 2011, thinkexist.com/quotation/talent_is_cheaper_than_table_salt-what_separates/220123.html.

Mamet, David. "Secret Names." In *The Best American Nonrequired Reading 2004*. Ed. Dave Eggers. Boston: Houghton Mifflin Harcourt, 2004.

Newkirk, Thomas, ed. *Nuts and Bolts: A Practical Guide to Teaching College Composition*. Portsmouth, NH: Boynton/Cook, 1993.

O'Connor, Flannery. "The Nature and Aim of Fiction." In *Mystery and Manners, Occasional Prose*. Ed. Sally Fitzgerald and Robert Fitzgerald. New York: Farrar, Straus and Giroux, 1969, 26th printing, 2000.

Partnership for 21st Century Skills. "Framework for 21st Century Learning," 2009. Accessed July 3, 2011, www.p21.org/index.php?option=com_content&task=view&id=254&Itemid=120.

Pirie, Bruce. *Reshaping High School English*. Urbana, IL: National Council of Teachers of English, 1997.

Proulx, Annie. "Inspiration? Head Down the Back Road, and Stop for the Yard Sales." *The New York Times*, May 10, 1999. Accessed June 12, 2012, partners.nytimes.com/library/books/051099proulx-writing.html.

Purves, Alan C., Joseph A. Quattrini, and Christine I. Sullivan. *Creating the Writing Portfolio: A Guide for Students*. Lincolnwood, IL: NTC Publishing Group, 1995.

Rosenblatt, Roger. "The Writer as Detective." *New York Times*, Sunday Section, July 8, 2011.

Smith, Walter "Red" Wellesley. Quote Investigator, September 14, 2011. Accessed January 21, 2012, quoteinvestigator.com/2011/09/14/writing-bleed.

Thoreau, Henry David. *Walden*, 150th Anniversary Edition. (Boston: Houghton Mifflin, 2004).

Toffler, Alvin, and John Hennessey. "Embracing the Need to Learn and Relearn." President's Column. *Stanford Magazine*, January/February 2002. Accessed August 8, 2012, alumni.stanford.edu/get/page/magazine/article/?article_id=38371.

Wallace, David Foster. "Tense Present: Democracy, English, and the Wars over Usage." In *Critical Encounters with Texts: Finding a Place to Stand*. Ed. Margaret Himley and Anne Fitzsimmons, 539–70. Boston: Pearson Custom Publishing, 2004.

Woolf, Virginia. "The Modern Essay," chapter 19. *The Common Reader*, eBooks@Adelaide, University of Adelaide, August 24, 2010, updated April 29, 2012. Accessed June 11, 2012, ebooks.adelaide.edu.au/w/woolf/virginia/w91c/chapter19.html.

Zmuda, Allison. "Springing into Active Learning." *ASCD Journal* 66, no. 3 (2008): 38–42.

About the Author

Nancy A. Dafoe is an award-winning published poet and fiction writer, in addition to being an English educator working and living in Central New York. She has taught in a variety of settings, including junior high school, high school, and college, and at different grade levels. Prior to teaching, Dafoe worked as a journalist and in public relations.

Dafoe currently teaches at East Syracuse Minoa Central High School in East Syracuse, New York, where she teaches AP English literature and composition, creative writing, and journalism. She previously taught freshman composition.